OUR UNSEEN GUEST

OUR UNSEEN GUEST

The Finley's Conversations with Stephen, 1920

Introduction by
Linda Pendleton

Linda Pendleton

Pendleton Artists
California

ISBN-13: 978-1478207665
ISBN-10: 1478207663

Cover Design by Judy Bullard

Printed and Bound in the United States of America
Create Space
100 Enterprise Way
Suite A 200
Scotts Valley, California 95066

"There is no death,
there is only change."
~Spirit Guide, Dr. Peebles,
To Dance With Angels by *Don and Linda Pendleton*

"There is another reality enfolding our—
as close as our breath!
~Don Pendleton (1927-1995)

INTRODUCTION

Since the 1700s, "Darby and Joan" have been considered to be a happily married, middle-aged couple living a quiet and uneventful life. Poems have been written, especially during Victorian times, referring to this imaginary couple.

But the Darby and Joan, authors of *Our Unseen Guest*, published in 1920, were hardly living an uneventful life. And it would be several years later before their true identity would be revealed.

The couple were professionals and had decided not to reveal their identities due to the subject matter of their book: conversations with an American soldier who died in World War I in France. They believed they could not risk their professional careers with the controversy their book was sure to bring. You see, Joan became a medium for this dead soldier. Over time he gave them information on life, and life after death and the continuation of consciousness.

So who was this mystery couple who were investigating what some consider to be the paranormal, while many others would consider their experiences to be extraordinary and awe-inspiring but within the norm of the human experience?

And who was this dead man who became known as "Stephen?"

Within the book, *Our Unseen Guest*, you will come to know who they were, and also you may learn more about life, life after death, and how consciousness lives on after the death of the physical body.

"Joan" was actually Ruth Ebright Finley. Ruth was born in 1884 in Akron, Ohio, daughter Dr. L.S. Ebright and his wife, Julia Ann Bissell. Her father was a physician and also at one time a postmaster of Akron. She studied at Oberlin in 1902, and the next term at Buchtel College but never completed her college degree.

After college she began a newspaper reporting career at the Akron *Beacon Journal*, and soon gained a name for herself. She moved on to the *Cleveland Press* and became know there for writing stories about working conditions of women. She was also credited with helping to get a bill passed to benefit working women.

It was at the *Cleveland Press* that she met Emmet Finley, an editor there. They were married soon after.

Emmet Finley was born in Salem, Ohio in 1881, son of Richard and Mary Barr Finley. In 1903, he received a degree from Adelbert College of Western Reserve and a law degree there in 1906. He was admitted to the Ohio bar in 1907.

He began a career as a newspaper reporter, editor, and held management positions in various newspaper printing and supply companies and organizations. He died in Dobbs Ferry, New York December 13, 1950.

Ruth Finley's career was varied. She worked as a reporter, editor of magazines and periodals, and was an historian, author and feminist. She wrote the book, *Old Patchwork Quilts and the Women Who Made Them*. She designed a quilt, "The Roosevelt Rose" given to first lady Eleanor Roosevelt, in 1938. In 1931, she published a biography, *The Lady of Godey's, Sarah Josepha Hale*.

But as I wrote above, the Finley's were not living an uneventful life. As they continued their careers, they were also exploring the paranormal. They do not identify the dead soldier by his real name because his family was still living and he apparently chose not to be identified, so they called him "Stephen." He had been an American volunteer soldier ambulance driver who had died in France during World War I, the year before the

Finley's contact with him began. Their book soon became a classic in spiritual literature of the time.

In recent years, after the death of Ruth Finley in 1955, it appears her papers revealed the identity of Stephen as being Richard Hall, an American soldier and Dartmouth graduate, who was killed on Christmas morning, 1915, by a German shell while driving an ambulance on a steep, shell-endangered road near Hartmanns-Weilerkopf. It is said that some of the bloodiest battles of the war were fought in that area.

At his funeral, according to the *New York Times*, the Cross of War was pinned upon the French Flag which covered his body. After attending Hall's funeral, Inspector General of the American Ambulance in the Field stated: "Hall was buried with honors of war in an Alsatian valley which once more belongs to France and in which our American ambulances are working among great green mountains and picturesque villages torn by shells and swarming with soldiers.

"His grave, in a crowded military cemetery, is next that of a French officer who fell the same morning. It bears the brief inscription: Richard Hall, an American who died for France.

"Simple mountain people in the only part of Germany where foreign soldiers are today brought to the grave many wreaths of native flowers and Christmas greens. These people have lived now for nearly a year and a half in danger of their own lives and in daily contact with the dead and dying. But the sacrifice of this modest, devoted young American has found a place in their hearts, and I was told by at least three families that they would keep flowers on the grave until the end of the war when they hoped the parents could visit it.

"Hall was killed by a stray shell at a lonely turn in the road up the mountain which German guns try intermittently to reach. His car was demolished and swept off the road. The shell struck him several hours before daybreak, and a number of his comrades crawled in ambulances up and down the mountain past the spot before early dawn revealed the occurrence.

"Luke Doyle, who at first was reported wounded at the same time, was in fact struck in the arm by shrapnel splinter four days before. The first aid station where he and other members of the Ambulance section were stationed was under fire, and everybody was forced to seek safety in a bomb-proof shelter, through the door of which a nearly spent splinter of a shell entered.

"The funeral for Hall was held in a little Protestant chapel, five miles down the valley, usually attended by many officers and soldiers and natives of the valley, but today reserved for Hall and his comrades, as the soldiers were on duty on the mountain crest where a fierce fight for Hartmanns-Weilerkopf still was waging.

"At the conclusion of the service Hall's citation was read and the Cross of War pinned on the coffin. The body was then carried to the cemetery by Lovering Hill, who commands his section, French officer, and English officer and Stephen Gallati, R. Matter, and Allyn Jennings, his comrade. His brother Louis Hall, walked directly behind the coffin, and sixteen solders, belonging to a battalion on leave from the trenches, marched in files on each side with arms reversed.

"Louis Hall was returned to Paris on his way back to the United States. He will take with him the riddled canvas side of the automobile ambulance which has been presented by Dartmouth students, and to the Alpha Delta Phi, the fraternity of which his brother was a member, he will give the steel helmet which Richard Hall wore when killed."

I first came to know of "Darby and Joan," and "Stephen," some years ago while reading the "Betty Books" written by Stewart Edward White. The "Betty Books" are considered classics within the literature of spirit communication. It was only after reading his three spiritual books that I become curious about his other literary works, and then discovered the richness of his legacy and his impact on the history of our country. I have recently written Introductions to several of his public domain books and published them in e-book format with nice cover illustrations.

More than one hundred years ago, White became a popular writer. He was a lover of nature: an explorer, conservationist, naturalist, and big game hunter. His love for nature, conservation, and adventure were to become very much a part of his literary works over his long career. Stewart once said his books, including his novels, were stories based upon actual experience. He loved writing about pioneers, the West, logging, and nature. Stewart's first book, *The Westerner* was published in 1901. He was twenty-eight years of age. That was the beginning of his successful literary career and he would go on to publish more than 50 books and short stories, including Westerns, pioneer and adventure stories, children stories, and nonfiction over his career that lasted until his death, September 18, 1946 in Hillsborough, California.

In 1937, Stewart Edward White published a nonfiction book that was very different then his previous popular books. It was an adventure, but not the kind he had written for nearly forty years. And again, like in many of his books, he wrote from personal experience. It would be the first of several books on the subject of spirit communication.

The story of his new book began March 17, 1919. It was on that evening when a small group of friends arrived at Stewart's home with a Ouija board. A woman present that evening, which he identifies as "Betty," had little interest in the spirit game but the board repeatedly spelled out her name. She was reluctant to join the "spirit reading" again, but the board then began to spell out repeatedly, "Get a pencil." Betty had no knowledge of automatic writing, but a few days later she did get a pencil and as she sat quietly, the pencil began to move across the paper without effort from her, nor did she have knowledge of what was being written. For the next few months, these "automatic writing sessions" with spirit took place. A year later, Betty was a full trance medium of a group of spirits who Stewart and Betty nicknamed *The Invisibles*. This remarkable book, *The Betty Book*, became the first of several books on the subject. The second book, *Across the Unknown* came out two years later and about the time the third book, *The Unobstructed Universe* was published in 1940, it was revealed that "Betty" was his wife, Elizabeth. Elizabeth had passed away in 1939, after twenty years of recording their experiences with the world of spirit. Although she left the physical body, Stewart continued to have contact with her from the other side, and wrote of those experiences in *The Unobstructed Universe* in which their friend "Joan" (Joan of Darby and Joan) is the medium for messages and teachings from Betty.

The "Betty Books" are considered classics within the literature of spirit communication, and it was the Betty Books that brought Stewart Edward White to my attention a few years ago. It was only after reading his three spiritual books that I become curious about his other literary works, and then discovered the richness of his legacy and his impact on the history of our country.

In these nonfiction books he treated their adventure into the world of spirit in very much the same way as he did all his other adventurous journeys throughout his life. The style of writing reflected that enthusiastic adventure and exploration, even though it was a journey into the unknown, into the self, and into the after life. He was able to write about the adventures beyond the veil in very much the same passionate way he wrote about nature and the earthly frontier.

Attempting to give the reader an idea of the credibility and importance of Betty's message from the spirit group, *The Invisibles*, he explained how psychic events have to be experienced in a personal way, yet he is saying that exposure to or reading about the spiritual experiences of others can be an exciting and fulfilling experience. So if out hiking the beautiful countryside, or listening to or reading channeled wisdom, both can be an exciting journey.

In his words from his nonfiction, *Across the Unknown*, Chapter VI, Landmarks:

"In a new country a man must find his own way. The landmarks planted by his predecessors he must discover for himself. When he overtakes them, he is heartened by their evidence that others have passed this way and found the way reliable. That is the principle reason for placing landmarks, against the time when someone shall need them.

"But also there is a value in travelers' tales. They excite interest. They breathe the atmosphere of adventure in strange lands. They awaken the romance of the unexplored and the unknown, arousing us to venture.

"Before commencing the records of Betty's exploration I must emphasize one thing every writer knows. No account does more than insignificant credit to the original. And this seems to be particularly true when we deal with the far reaches of the mind. A kind of penumbra of illumination accompanies the thing itself, which is lacking in cold type. I suppose this is inevitable when we concern ourselves with a reality whose greater part is intangible, beyond the measuring ability of the brain. I cannot sufficiently stress this apparently obvious statement. Only personal experience can realize its import."

Stewart Edward White died September 18, 1946 at Hillsborough, California, where he had lived for many years. A nonfiction book completed days before his death, *With Folded Wings* was published in 1947, and another nonfiction manuscript, *The Job of Living* was published in 1948.

The legacy left to us by Stewart Edward White lives on, and nearly sixty-five years later, his works are still appreciated as they were at the opening of the twentieth century.

In *The Unobstructed Universe*, White writes of their first meeting with Darby and Joan in 1922 at the home of American writer, playwright, and medium, Margaret Cameron. Also present was another psychic, Lucy Lamont Gavit, wife of John Palmer Gavit who was managing editor and director of the *New York Evening Post*. Over the next 17 years the White's had only spent time with Darby and Joan on two occasions, and that apparently was because they lived on different coast.

A year after the death of Elizabeth (Betty) White, Stewart went east to visit with Darby and Joan, and it was there that his wife immediately began to communicate through the mediumship of Joan.

As it turned out, Betty had plenty to say, and over the following months she not only gave fascinating information and teachings, some of it confirming the spiritual philosophy of Stephen, but also enhancing and adding to his ideas.

Stephen also came through Joan's channeling, and at times there was a mutual ongoing dialogue with both Stephen and Betty from the other side.

In explaining more about the other side and consciousness, on one occasion Betty reminded Darby through Joan, that Stephen had over and over again told Darby that his first job there on the other side had been to meet boys who died suddenly in the war and without having the little interim between the two consciousnesses because of sudden death, would then explain to them what happened and where they were. That information from Stephen had been years before, prior to the publication of *Our Unseen Guest*.

The unseen guest of the Finley's told his earth friends that consciousness is the one and only reality. And from his point of view, consciousness exists, here and on the other side.

So enjoy your exploration of the mystery of life after death.

~Linda Pendleton
California, 1-11-2011

Our Unseen Guest

"If a man die, shall he live again?" Job 14:14

Dedication

TO MY comrades in khaki who asked, as I too asked: "Will I come back, and, if I do not, will there be a me and where will I go?". . . .

To THOSE who loved me so truly that they sent me into the front rank of fighters for the great peace: My mother whose far-seeing motherhood reaches out to protect yet unborn generations; my father whose soul is of that strength which, visioning, dares to sacrifice; my brother who marched beside me. . . .

To THEM that went and to them that waited, to all laying their best of self and of love upon the altar of universal freedom. ...

I, "STEPHEN," who have gone over the top of life to victory, dedicate this book—in answer to their wistful questionings and as a call to that wider service which shall embrace all time, all space, all being.

I

THE COMING OF STEPHEN

Our first experience with psychic phenomena occurred on the evening of December 7, 1916—by way of a ouija-board. Neither Joan nor I had ever seen a ouija-board before. The "toy" came into our hands quite by accident.

We were taking our dinners at a private boarding-house some blocks from the apartment building in which we lived. On the evening in question a sudden storm blew off the lake, while we were at table, and after the meal Joan and I wandered into a deserted sitting-room to wait until the wind and sleet abated. There one of the resident guests had left the ouija, a remnant doubtless of some Halloween party.

"How does the thing work?" Joan asked. I read the directions; we rested the board, whereon the alphabet was printed in two semicircles, upon our knees, and put the tips of our fingers on the flatiron-like pointer.

"Now," said I, "this tripod affair is supposed to move from letter to letter, spelling out a message."

Thus we sat for a period—ten minutes, perhaps. We joked, I remember, of the good fortunes ouija would tell us. But no message came.

Then, just as we were about to give up, the tripod began to move.

"Quality of consciousness," it spelled. A pause—then, once more, "Quality of consciousness."

"Darby!" Joan took her fingers from the pointer. "You can't fool me like that. You did it!' Quality of consciousness'—that doesn't mean anything, anyway."

I looked into Joan's eyes. Was it she who had moved the tripod, or did she honestly accuse me?

"Not guilty!" I pleaded. For a moment we faced each other in silence. Then said Joan, gravely, "Let's try it again." So we tried it again.

On the instant the tripod gathered strength. Over the alphabet it moved, slowly, yet with machine-like precision, pausing on this letter and that. Here are the words it spelled: "For you two I have a message, a revelation. Communication is so slow, so difficult, that I can do little more than give you the suggestion. But if you will reason along the lines I point out, you can reach the truth."

"What truth?"

"In as far," the answer came, "as it is given you to understand, that ultimate truth—the why, the whence, the whither—which men have longed to know since knowledge was."

"Who are you?" I asked, addressing the empty air.

"I am Robert L , an American," the tripod spelled, giving the last name, though it is not set down here.

"Robert L ?" I said, the name meaning nothing to me. "Is that right—Robert L?"

"L ," spelled the ouija-board. Then came, not Robert, but another Christian name —Stephen, let us say, though the name actually spelled began, like Robert, with R. "We understand your family name to be L ," I said. "Now can you straighten out the given name? Is it Robert or Stephen?"

Promptly the ouija-board spelled a contraction, itself not beginning with R, of the name for which "Stephen" is here substituted—a contraction or nickname, by which (I anticipate my story) he whom this narrative will continue to call Stephen had been known among his friends.

"Your name, then, is Stephen L ?" I asked. "Yes," replied the ouija-board.

To Joan and me Stephen's name, which we do not feel at liberty to divulge, meant nothing more, on this night of December 7, 1916, than any totally new name signifies when stumbled across for the first time. We had never heard of such a person.

The margin of the newspaper on which I had been recording the ouija-board's words threatened to prove inadequate. I dug an envelope out of my pocket, and said: "We don't know you. But never mind that. Go ahead."

"Let me tell you about myself," the tripod answered.

And then to our great amazement there was written out upon the ouija-board the death story of a soldier, an American killed in service of the Allied cause. Not once, except as I removed my hands to record the sentences, did the tripod hesitate. Joan and I sat astounded at the mere facility of the performance. The circumstantial vividness of the tripod's story was dumfounding, for, like Stephen's name, the story of his death was wholly new to us.

Why is the story not given here? Because Stephen wishes it withheld; because to those still in this life whom he loved, and loves, undesired publicity would result. His death was unique; to report the story of the ouija-board would be to identify him.

It is curious; already I speak of Stephen as though he were a person, as real a person as myself. This manner of speech, is a convenience, at least. As a matter of fact, Joan and I do not wish here and now to pass judgment definitely on Stephen's reality—or unreality.

I said to Stephen some weeks later: "You wish us to make public your philosophy. Do you realize that the story of your death is a logical part of any report we might make? Verified, it is evidential, tending to prove that, dead though you are, you still live."

It was not Stephen who answered, but another, one who came in Stephen's wake, hopeful, apparently, that he might be of help, now and then, in clarifying a doubtful philosophic point. Let us call this personality "the professor." The professor's answer was: "Stephen's revelation is its own best test. Its reasonableness, my dear sir, in the light of earth's already acquired knowledge, is its best proof."

Yet something of Stephen's story, as spelled by the ouija-board, I am permitted to tell— its atmosphere, shorn of identifying facts. First came a picture of war's horror, painted with an intimacy one might expect only from an eye-witness. "Millions," the tripod spelled, "have already fallen. And the suffering and the wounds!"

Stephen spoke of the dead and the dying and of "those maimed, those who must still exist through years of weariness and discouragement, not knowing that therein lies their great chance."

I am not at liberty to state the nature of Stephen's service in the Allied army nor to specify the mission that cost him his life. That mission, as described by the tripod, was one of the greatest danger; it sent him out into the night alone.

The tripod spelled: "There was a mist in the air—half mist, half smoke from the battle that had been raging for days up and down the mountain.

A call came. . . . The dark was of a blackness that could be felt, and it was cold. ... I am not ashamed to say that I was afraid.. . . All day we had been under fire. ... I hummed a tune under my breath for company and to keep my courage up. Several shells burst ahead of me. ... I went on. . . I was singing when the shell that sent me into eternity, as I now know it, hit."

The rest of Stephen's story is quoted without omissions:

"I went out, out, out, out. I can find no words to tell you the horror of sudden death. It is the one great tragedy. When thought returned, I was as one lost in a familiar yet wholly strange world. Aimlessly I wandered, seeking I knew not what, dazed, mystified. I did not know I was, as you say and as I used to say, dead.

"When death comes naturally there are always those here to meet the voyagers. But there was no one to meet me, no one to explain that I had graduated into a new plane of consciousness.

"At last one came, a woman, a very sweet woman whose service here has done much to alleviate the shock of battle-field graduation, and took me by the—shall I say, hand?—and led me to a—may I say, quiet woodland spot?—where after a time I learned the hope, the reality of the triumphant blessing I had achieved.

"And so I have chosen my work here, and with that work I go on—the comforting of those who come to us suddenly out of the shock of battle. I meet them, poor frightened soldier-boys, and teach them the truth —the simplicity of their own immortality."

II
SUBCONSCIOUS MINDS

AT the word "immortality" the tripod bewilderment at the foolish bits of wood, while I finished my notes. With the striking of a clock she jerked her hands from the tripod. Not until we reached home did we venture discussion of the evening's happening.

"What do you suppose does it?" I asked.

"The easy explanation," my wife answered, "would be—*you*. Have you all that story down?"

"Another easy explanation," said I, "would be—*you*. Yes, I think I have that story down."

From out one pocket I took my newspaper, its margins covered with Stephen's words. From another I hauled a heterogeneous mass of old envelops, likewise scribbled over with the ouija-board's spellings. Then I fished up a dozen or so of Joan's cards, which I had gleaned from her purse to eke out my paper supply.

"There is no use trying to unravel this jumble to-night," I decided. "I'll piece the stuff together to-morrow and type it at the office."

This on the morrow I did. And that evening, in our own familiar living-room, Joan and I studied the detail of the ouija-board's strange spellings.

I looked up from reading Stephen's death story aloud, and saw Joan searching out, with shifting, sidewise glance, a shadowy corner of the room, whither the light of our lamp scarcely penetrated; and I knew the eerie feeling that was in her soul. For, with Stephen spelling himself out of and then back into existence, the far corners had assumed for me, too, an uncomfortable fascination. It seemed that our ghost who spelled so well might also walk.

"Darby," said Joan, "you *must* have made that story up."

"Joan," I said, "you made it up yourself."

Thus we had it back and forth that evening and for several days. I knew that Stephen's name had never entered my thought until I read it from the ouija-board, and I knew I had never heard or seen anything similar to Stephen's story of his passing out. So I said to Joan, "You did it," sure in my heart she had done no such thing.

And she, wishing, like myself, to skirt the supernatural, said, "No, Darby, you did it," though she knew I had not.

In the end, of course, we, whose custom it is to tell each other the truth, admitted the easy explanation would not suffice. Together we faced the fact of a something unexplained. Not for a moment, however, did we accept Stephen for what he purported to be.

"The phenomenon doubtless is genuine," I said. "Because it is genuine, it's explainable, and that without the aid of a dead man willing to spend his immortality writing on a childish toy. But why should you and I bother? Would it not be best for us just to forget this Stephen and his dying?"

"Let's," Joan answered. "The thing's creepy."

"I suppose," I went on, "that if there ever was such a person as Stephen, I could run the facts of him down."

"I wouldn't," said Joan. "Let's just do as you said—forget him."

And yet before another day passed Joan had bought a ouija-board.

When I came home from the office she led me into a closet off the living-room, where stood a trunk. Behind the trunk she had secreted her purchase. And there, when our toy was not in use, we would hide it. Often of evenings, if the door-bell rang, we would get the ouija-board back into its hiding-place just in time for us to welcome the caller with uncompromised faces. "There were two sizes," said Joan, as she exhibited her purchase. "I bought the big one."

"But why did you buy any? I thought we agreed to forget Stephen."

"And we shall," she answered. "I don't care anything about Stephen. But I do want to know what 'quality of consciousness' means. I can't get the phrase out of my head."

That night, for the second time, Joan and I placed our fingers on a ouija-board's pointer. Again came Stephen; and immediately he began a system of thought so foreign to either of us that I could not accuse Joan even in pretense, nor she me, of its production. Before a week had passed such conversations as the following were ordinary.

"The world is ready for the truth," spells Stephen. "There are many who will be rejoiced to believe, if you but tell them. The time is ripe for the revelation."

"And why ripe now?" I ask.

"Because," Stephen answers, "never before, since man's own scientific knowledge has been developed to a point enabling him to understand the revelation now planned, has it been possible for the higher degrees of consciousness here to communicate with correspondingly high degrees on your side. Such communication is possible now because, owing to the vast slaughter of the war, so much of consciousness still close to earth is on my plane. As a result our potentiality here for the purpose of communication is strengthened, while earth's collected consciousness, strained by the upheaval of a world war, is rendered unusually sensitive.

"Listen! The time is ripe. The world is waiting for a reasonable peg on which to hang its faith."

It was engrossing—the Stephen philosophy. That which Stephen had to say seemed so much more important than the question of who or what Stephen might be, that in a way we did just what Joan said we would: We forgot him. The "quality of consciousness" quite overshadowed its expositor.

Then gradually the personality of this thing claiming to be a living dead man began to assert itself, built out of modesty, kindliness, droll wit, and piercing directness of understanding. From a vague unknown, Stephen became a well-recognized friend, a sort of correspondent we had never seen, whose letters nonetheless envisaged him. He was not really Stephen, of course. Impossible that he should be a discarnate intelligence! Even if he were, how could the fact be proved—by what evidence? Supported by the professor, by this time an occasional visitor at the board, Stephen himself echoed our question: How, by what evidence?

Said the professor: "If I should appear to your physical eye, if I sat down and talked to your physical ear, you would call me an hallucination."

Said Stephen: "If I told you facts, dates, names, and places you did not know, and subsequently you ascertained their truth, you would have tested nothing. You would say you had learned them long ago and forgotten them. If they concerned events happening as I spoke, you would say you received them telepathically from unknown, yet definite, earth personalities. As for prophecy, we here, rightly apprehended, are not soothsayers."

I think, though, that, in spite of Stephen and the professor, we would have sought to verify the soldier's name the ouija-board had given us, and the death story, had it not been for an odd, yet human, mental quirk; Joan and I did not want to catch this Stephen of the ouija-board, this friend of ours, up in an untruth. Investigation, we believed, would result in just that.

But it was one thing to regard Stephen simply as a phenomenon, dismissing the question of who or what might be the antecedent of that phenomenon. It was a more difficult thing so to regard Stephen's philosophy, once we realized the wonder of it. We could not avoid asking ourselves this question: Where did Stephen's elaborate system of thought originate?

It was not my conscious mind that was evolving the philosophy, nor was it Joan's. Of this we were certain. Was it, then, our subconscious minds—mine, Joan's, or a blending of the two?

Here was a plausible solution, one which, though it seemed forced, fortified us against the supernatural. And, so fortified, we dared finally to consider the possibility that Stephen, after all, might be quite what he said he was.

There were times—at night when the lights were low and the shadows many—when I said to Joan: "Stephen is real. He is an intelligence outside our own. Once he lived here; now he lives there; and he returns to help us, perhaps through us to help others." And Joan would nod and say, "It is a comprehensive explanation."

Morning! The world is awake, with men going sanely about their all-important tasks.

I say to Joan: "It's as plain as sunlight that Stephen is our subconscious minds. Men in their sleep have solved mathematical problems that for days baffled their conscious minds. The ouija-board is that little distraction of the conscious needed to set the subconscious free. It is the watch-charm with which the lecturer must toy if his hour is to go smoothly. Stephen's words are the creation of that part of our thought which operates outside the focus of concentration."

Then, quite sure of the mystery's solution, we would take the ouija-board upon our laps, and I would say: "Stephen, you are my subconscious mind."

Stephen's answer would be: "The subconscious self and the quality of consciousness are closely related. Because of that close relation I can communicate with you. But they are not the same."

And so Joan and I vacillated—sure only of one thing, that we were both averagely normal minded.

Day by day we had been accustomed to go about our work with healthy enjoyment in its successful performance—work far removed from participation or even interest in transcendental mysteries. To be sure, we took it for granted that modern living had progressed far beyond the generally accepted standards of conventionalized thought; yet as between time-tested teachings and the "isms" that infest the day, we preferred the former. With the "isms" we had had no contact.

Sure of ourselves, then, we felt privileged to vacillate. Stephen might be this or might be that. He might be the soul of one departed from this world of nature, yet living forward in a world of supernature. He might be a creature of our own unconscious making. Confident of our own integrity, we held any explanation permissible. Indeed, what matter if we failed to explain this Stephen at all?

Ill

A QUESTION OF IDENTITY

"I WAS decorated by France. You can find my record in 'The Story of the Red Cross,' possibly. . . ." (Here another title was given, which I withhold lest it identify Stephen.) "A book—I cannot quite tell the name—recently published, and to be had at any bookstore."

These words were spelled by Stephen on the evening of January 15, 1917.

The next day Joan visited a bookstore. No one there had ever heard of "The Story of the Red Cross." Nor was any book, bearing the other title Stephen had given, known.

"That clinches the matter," Joan said to me. "It's subconscious mind, Darby. But whose? Not mine, surely. Yours, I suppose. Yet this philosophy of Stephen's—how unlike you!"

"The subconscious-mind theory is most convincing," I answered, "until connected with either you or me. Stephen's philosophy is beyond the two of us put together."

A day or so later Joan again was in the bookstore, her work taking her there occasionally. The owner came to her and said he thought he knew what book she had been looking for. A volume, new to Joan, was handed her. It bore a title differing from either of the titles Stephen had given, but related to both in sense. Joan leafed through it, called me at the office, and asked if I could come to the store. I went. She handed me the book, new to me as to her, and asked me to turn to such and such a page.

And there, in black and white, was the story of Stephen L , of his service in the Allied army, and of his death. There were the facts the ouija-board had told us on the night of December 7,1916. Had we been investigators searching for proof of the survival of personality after death, with what more challenging evidence could we have been confronted? Stephen of the ouija-board had demonstrated there actually was a Stephen L , an American, killed in the service of the Allied cause at such and such a place, on such and such a date and in such and such a way.

We were not elated, however. We who had feared lest we catch Stephen up in an untruth were frightened now by his very truthfulness.

Wherein was the occurrence extraordinary?

Something on the night of December 7, 1916, caused a ouija-board to spell for Joan and me, "I am Stephen L." The same something caused the ouija-board to spell what purported to be the facts of Stephen L 's death.

On January 15, 1917, something prompted the ouija-board to direct us to look for a certain book. We looked, found the book, and therein was the story of a real Stephen L , how he had died, and when and where; and the statements of this story were the same as those of the narrative that had been spelled out on the ouija-board over a month before.

Obviously the chain of circumstances is extraordinary only in the event that Joan and I, prior to December 7, 1916, were ignorant of

Stephen L . We have testified to that ignorance. To the best of our knowledge and belief we were ignorant, not only of the death of Stephen L , but of his ever having lived.

Of what are these extraordinary circumstances evidence? On what basis can they be explained?

Four possible explanations suggest themselves. They are:

1. Guess.
2. Telepathy.
3. The subconscious-mind theory.
4. The spiritistic theory.

And at least one other explanation might be offered—the cosmic-mind theory. But this, it would seem, is pure theory, having neither traditional nor experimental backing. Perhaps it can be best discussed later, in the light of Stephen's philosophy.

Is not the "guess" explanation hopeless? Joan and I were not guessing that night of December 7, 1916. We were not doing anything of which we were aware, save that, while waiting for the storm to stop, we sat with our fingers resting on a piece of wood. Yet granted we were guessing and didn't know it, granted one or the other of us unconsciously chanced the opinion that there was once a person named Stephen L , and that he was killed in the course of military service in Europe, would it not have been an impossible coincidence that our guess, wholly without foundation, should have proved true, not simply in a general way, but in detail?

Was telepathy at the root of the occurrence? Was the thought of some person here on earth to whom Stephen was known transferred in strange fashion to Joan and me as we sat at the ouija-board? Granted thought can and does transfer itself from one person to another through channels other than the senses, is it conceivable that so circumstantial a story as that of Stephen's death was thus transferred —accurately?

The subconscious-mind theory has already caused us to pause; even in the present case it must, I feel, arrest most thoughtful consideration. This theory implies that, though Joan and I had no conscious knowledge of Stephen L , his existence and death had, as a matter of fact, been brought to our attention prior to December 7, 1916; that we forgot what we had known; and that in some way or other the ouija-board called this knowledge back into conscious thought. This seems unlikely.

Stephen L had been dead only a matter of months. If Joan and I, or one of us, once knew of his death, how brief a time had been required to wipe the fact clean from our memories!

Concerning the spiritistic theory I shall say at this time only that Stephen's philosophy, which is the primary theme of this record, goes to the entire question of the possibility and reasonableness of survival after death.

It was a startling test Stephen had given us. Yet when the shock of it had passed we found ourselves still vacillating, though there was an added difficulty: Up to the day of Stephen's identification we could, when so inclined, dismiss him as a mere fiction. With Stephen thus out of the way, we were free to regard his philosophy as the product of our own subconsciousness. This explanation of the mystery we might, and assuredly did, doubt, yet there was no external evidence to the contrary. Now we had to square with the subliminal theory, not only Stephen's philosophy, but Stephen himself. How accept the thought that we once knew of Stephen L yet forgot that knowledge so completely that even the anomaly of its writing itself out on the ouija-board failed to refresh our memories?

IV

A PUZZLED FRIEND

OUR dilemma was so puzzling that, despite the lack of confidence Stephen and the professor had expressed in evidential messages, Joan and I welcomed a chance happening that resulted in further tests. One night, as we were deep in the philosophy, the telephone rang; Joan stepped from the room to answer. While she was at the 'phone, the door-bell rang; and I, neglecting first to hide the ouija-board, admitted a caller. Let's call him F. W.

Just as F. W. entered, Joan returned. She seized the board and tripod, and rushed toward the closet with its protecting trunk, but too late.

"That's a ouija-board," accused F. W.

"Ever see one before?" I asked.

Yes, F. W. had—once. When he was a youngster, he said, there was a freak (his word) family—neighbors of his family—who had cultivated ouija with great seriousness, His mother had attended one of the meetings and taken him along.

"But what in the name of common sense," F. W. asked, "are you two doing with a ouija-board?"

We told how, by accident, we ran across the toy at the boarding-house, adding that for the sake of amusement we had bought the outfit he now saw.

"If there's any fun to be had out of the contraption," said F. W., "let's have it."

And so, with F. W. as spectator and stenographer, Joan and I made ready for the "fun." We should have known better than to have left Stephen out of our calculations. He would have none of our frivolity, but instead insisted on continuing his philosophical discussion. The conversation F. W. recorded follows:

Darby: F. W. is with us, Stephen.

Stephen: Your friend.

Darby: Have you a message for F. W.?

Stephen: Later. I am glad he is here. Joan, Darby, and F. W. have much the same degree of consciousness. Therein is the friendship explained. I would like F. W. to take this affair as seriously as he can. Let's go on with the discussion. Quality of consciousness, I have told you, we have at birth; quantity is developed. Degree of consciousness is made up of the possession of quality and quantity. Suppose you discuss this with me. I want you to understand thoroughly.

What did F. W. know about the quality and quantity of consciousness! He did know that his curiosity was piqued. And, of course, he accused Joan and me of being the true operators of the tripod.

"Why try to fool me?" he demanded.

"That's what Joan used to say to me," I answered, "and what I said to her. But we have fought that all out. We know now that, consciously at least, we have nothing more to do with the movements of the ouija-board's pointer than you have."

"Bet you can't do the trick blindfolded," said F. W.

"Bet we can't, either," said Joan.

So F. W. blindfolded us. I could see nothing, and Joan says she couldn't. We placed our hands upon the tripod. Slowly it moved; whether to a purpose or not we did not know until F. W. began calling out the letters. Here is what the tripod spelled:

"This is harder. There is a psychic, a receiving station, here. She will remember having had the experience of feeling that some one was standing behind her and of turning to find nothing."

Then came a pause, then more movements. These, F. W. complained, were incoherent. He begged just one more sentence; and finally the ouija-board replied with the following: "Is hate enough?" (Which meant, I suppose, that Stephen disliked the test.) ·

The blindfolds were removed, and F. W. suggested that he and I try to run the board. We tried, but without result, other than that the tripod moved aimlessly back and forth. Then Joan proposed that she and F. W. take the board in hand. They did, with success. The movements were slower than with Joan and me, and the course from letter to letter was not so direct; but the words were spelled with equal distinctness.

"I would rather go on with the discussion," Stephen said. "Darby!"

"You want Darby?" asked F. W.

"Yes," answered Stephen. "He understands better."

F. W. took his hands from the tripod, leaned back in his chair, and exclaimed, "Fair enough!" This phrase he uses frequently, to express either agreement or surprise. In the present instance it expressed both. F. W. did not understand, and he was bewildered.

"I think you two were both blindfolded so that you could not see anything," he said, after a bit. "Just the same, let me blindfold you again. And in addition I want you to turn your faces as far away from the board as possible."

In the midst of F. W.'s speech Joan and I had again put our fingers on the tripod. It was in motion before F. W. could finish.

"The blindfold is undignified," it spelled. "Such things are of no importance in the scheme of things. I have given you tests enough."

But F. W. insisted—and certainly Joan and I were very much interested in his experiment. With great care he adjusted the handkerchiefs to our eyes. We turned our faces as far from the board as we could. Neither of us saw anything; it would have been impossible, F. W. agreed when the experiment was over.

With everything in readiness, F. W. said: "Now this time I am not going to call out the letters. I shall put them all down, and after the handkerchiefs are removed I'll read you the result, if there is any."

It seemed as though Joan and I sat blindfolded for half an hour, though F. W. said later the time was only about five minutes. We could feel the tripod moving over the board. I wondered if it wouldn't run clear off, but it didn't. Every now and then F. W. would speak, as though to Stephen, thus indicating that a result of some sort was being achieved. Finally the blindfolds were removed. I report the ouija-board's spellings together with F. W.'s questions:

F. W.: Why are you talking to Joan and Darby?

Stephen: To give them the revelation which I first mentioned to them at Jevon's.

F. W. (to whom the name Jevon was without meaning): Repeat the words following " which."

Stephen: I first mentioned to them at Jevon's.

F. W.: What does the last word mean?

Stephen: To Darby, eat.

F. W.: You are ungrammatical. "To Darby eat" is just nonsense.

It is understood that ouija-board spellings are in the nature of things unpunctuated. But even punctuation might have failed to make the cryptic phrase plain to F. W. Several times he repeated his opinion that the words "to Darby eat" were incoherent. Joan and I remember the jerkiness, expressive of impatience, with which Stephen at last made the following reply:

"Jennie Jevon keeps a boarding-house."

Mrs. Jevon did keep the boarding-house at which Joan and I took our dinners and at which we first met Stephen. F. W. knew we dined out, but did not know the name of the woman who to Darby meant "eat"; hence his confusion. Was Mrs. Jevon's first name Jennie? Neither Joan nor I could be sure we had ever heard her given name.

It was a mystified F. W. that bade us good night, close to one o'clock in the morning.

"I don't get this thing at all," he said, as he pulled on his overcoat. "But give me another chance. It's intensely interesting. What are you two going to do to-morrow evening— Friday?"

We regretted an engagement. "But," said Joan, "we'll be waiting right here for you Saturday evening."

Our Friday engagement, it chanced, fell through. And so I telephoned F. W.'s home. When told he was not there, I called several places where I thought he might be. F. W. was not to be found.

"Oh, well," said Joan, "let's do some testing on our own hook."

We took the ouija-board upon our laps. In an instant Stephen was at hand, announcing his presence as usual by spelling his name.

"Stephen," I said, "we are going to test you folks out a trifle to-night. I want you to let me talk to some one I knew in this life."

"I'll do the testing," Stephen replied. "Surely you realize the importance of my revelation. If I make the survival of consciousness after what you call death reasonable in the light of your own knowledge, what greater evidence can there be?"

Joan and I were determined, though. So, too, apparently was Stephen. The tripod began what seemed a dance. First it lifted itself up on the two rear legs; then, on one rear leg and the front leg. Then Stephen would come for a second, spell, "Silly," then disappear. After a [moment he would spell, "Stupid," and again disappear. Then for a long while the pointer remained motionless. At last it began to move, but with great uncertainty, as though operated by an unpractised hand.

"Not Stephen," it spelled, with many false starts and pauses. "Do you remember the time I stole your shirt? You cussed hard enough, because you were going to call on a girl."

"At one period of my life," I answered, "there were several persons who made good their linen needs from my drawer."

"Yes," said the ouija-board, "but only one of those persons is where I now am. I can be more specific. Do you remember the time I set up a joke on you, took forty dollars from your pocket?"

It seemed there could be no doubt that, if the speaker were other than my own subconscious mind, it was one whom I shall call Fred Q. For a few months before my marriage Fred Q. and I roomed together. He, like others living in the same house, had occasionally "borrowed" my clean shirts, just as I, when necessity warranted, had borrowed theirs. And I did remember the time he had taken forty dollars from my pocket. Joan's subconscious mind was absolved. There isn't a chance in the world that she had ever been told the absurd tale of the shirt or that of the forty dollars.

To cap the climax, the ouija-board next spelled, "Gunboats."

It was laughable. Fred Q. had insisted on wearing shoes of a size even more than comfortably large. "Gunboats!" I used to exclaim, as I would wake up in the morning and see his shoes sprawling beside his bed. Here again Joan, conscious or subconscious, could not be accused. Either it was I, the subconscious me, who had spelled that word "gunboats," or—could it possibly have been Fred O., dead then something over a year?

Granted the shirt, the forty dollars, and the gunboats were really the work of my own subconsciousness, why, if it was necessary for my subconsciousness to spell anything, had it chosen these trivial memories of Fred Q.? For four or five years prior to his death I had seen little of him. In fact, he passed out of my life when Joan came in.

Stephen returned finally. "Did the test satisfy you?" he asked. "Or have you now just something more to explain?"

"Something more to explain away," was my answer.

"But surely," Stephen replied. "So why waste time? Let us go on with the revelation."

And then there began the unfolding of a new section of that which, to Joan and me, has seemed, quite as the ouija-board insisted, the most wonderful of tests—Stephen's philosophy, fully as unique in its purport as in the manner of its coming.

V

Uncle Michael

JOAN had promised F.W. he would find us waiting for him. Instead, when we reached home the next night, F. W. was waiting for us, with knowing mien.

"I tried to get you on the 'phone last night," I said. "I telephoned everywhere."

"Everywhere," he answered, "except the Public Library. I was doing a little reading, sort of sizing up this psychic stuff." He found his own way to the coat-closet. "I know the answer to that," he announced with assurance, as he caught sight of the ouija-board resting on the top of the trunk. "Take me into your confidence," said I. "Simple enough!" he replied. "It's subconscious mind. That ouija-board didn't spell a word night before last that wasn't either in your mind or Joan's or both."

"I don't believe either of us knew that Mrs. Jevon's first name was Jennie," said Joan. "We made inquiry, and Jennie it is."

"Well, you probably did know," answered F.W. "You forgot it—that's all. Right there's the point of the subconscious mind. We think we forget a lot of things that later we discover tucked away in our memory. I'll tell you what, though—the way you two ran the ouija-board blindfolded was remarkable."

"Does the subconscious mind explain that?" I asked.

"I wouldn't be surprised if it does," F. W. replied. "Think of the sleep-walker. The sleep-walker strolls safely through the most dangerous places. He climbs ladders, walks along the edge of cliffs, and all that sort of thing, guided not by sight, but by subliminal memories."

The sanity of F. W.'s attitude was contagious—would have been had not Joan and I sat night after night and seen an attention arresting system of philosophic thought build itself up out of what seemed to be nothing, each succeeding thought coherent with that which had gone before, each new development resting on a previously laid foundation. Subconscious mind? Perhaps. But when had Joan and I stored in our subconsciousness the material out of which, without effort, we were now building this structure of thought? And then there was Stephen of the ouija-board, who seemingly had proved to be Stephen L!

Telepathy, F. W. might have said, had he known how Stephen had identified himself. I do not think he would have charged Stephen's identification up to subconscious mind. For F. W.'s daily work and training, like Joan's and mine, fits one to remember dramatic facts and the names they involve. He would have appreciated the likelihood of our remembering a story such as Stephen L 's, once it came to our notice, the certainty we could not have forgotten such a story so completely that even the unusualness of its bobbing up on a ouija-board failed, wholly failed, to refresh our memories.

Suppose F. W. had said, telepathy. Thereby he would have asserted that on the night of December

7, 1916, some person—just who this person was Joan and I might never be able to ascertain—had turned over in his mind certain facts of Stephen L 's existence and death, and Joan and I—from a distance how great we might never be able to ascertain—had intercepted that person's thought in great detail and with exact accuracy. All this F. W. would have asserted despite the fact that he could not have cited from his own experience, or observation, a single other instance of telepathy, however sketchy.

Well, Joan and I took our positions at the ouija-board, F. W. again undertaking to make the record. Almost immediately this came, without hesitancy, but slowly:

"F. W., I am here. Recognize by personality. The day was cold. A country road. Two teams. We met your mother at the station. She came to spend the holidays and take you back. Who am I?"

"I don't recall any such incident," said F. W. "I don't know who you are."

"Runaway," spelled the ouija-board.

"Did the runaway have anything to do with an embankment?" asked F. W.

"River—bridge," spelled the ouija-board.

"Hello there!" exclaimed F. W. "Is this Uncle Michael?"

"Mouth-organ," replied the ouija-board.

"Now you are absurd," said F. W., nettled at the triviality of the ouija-board's last word. "Uncle Michael, the family never believed your horses ran away. They always thought you were the victim of foul play, robbers, maybe."

"No foul play," spelled the ouija-board. "Another team from the opposite curve. It was already running away. It ran into my off horse. The driver was drunk. When he saw the result he was so frightened he went on and kept silence."

"What had you hauled to market in your wagon?" asked F. W.

"Lumber," replied the ouija-board, then added: "I am not sure, but I think grain."

"You contradict yourself," said F. W.

"Elderberry whistle," replied the ouija-board.

The tripod stopped, and, much as F. W. insisted, there was no further word from Uncle Michael.

The facts of Uncle Michael's death, as F. W. told them to Joan and me, were these. He had lived in a distant state, on the farm where he and his sister, F. W.'s mother, had been reared. One day— F. W. at the time was a young boy— Uncle Michael started to market, driving a team of trusted horses. Night failed to bring him home. The next day his body was found at the foot of an embankment, the approach to a bridge a few miles from the farm. The team, trailing the wagon with broken harness, browsed in a fence-corner.

The obvious explanation was that the horses had run away; and the family had been unable to prove otherwise. But they had never accepted this explanation; Uncle Michael had known every inch of the road, and the horses he drove were reliable. His family believed he had been attacked by robbers, his body thrown over the embankment as a blind, and the horses deliberately frightened. The proceeds of his trip to market offered a motive for the crime. It happened, though, that Uncle Michael, contrary to his custom, had banked the money.

When F. W. made ready to bid Joan and me good night, the hour, as on the previous evening, was late. His assurance had vanished; amazement repossessed him. For here again were facts unknown to Joan and me, yet spelled out on our ouija-board.

The picture of Uncle Michael taking F. W. on a cold ride over a country road to meet his mother could be dismissed; F. W. remembered no such ride. And what of the two teams? One would hardly suppose it required two teams to carry one small boy to meet his mother. Yet in the death story, unrelated as it was to F. W.'s ride, there were, curiously, two teams, just as there was a country road. One could but smile at Uncle Michael's failure to remember whether it was lumber or grain he had hauled to town the day of his death. F. W. himself did not know what his uncle's wagon had contained. The "mouth-organ" and "elderberry whistle" remarks, Joan and I agreed with F. W., were too trivial to mean anything.

Despite discrepancies, however, and despite trivialities, the fact remained that the ouija-board had suggested to F. W. the personality of his dead Uncle Michael. At the time, neither Joan nor I knew there had ever been such a person as Uncle Michael.' We knew nothing of the family of F. W.'s mother, herself dead—who they, were or where they lived. F. W. realized our complete ignorance. How, he demanded, was he to attribute Uncle Michael to Joan's or my subconscious mind?

"Might it not have been your subconscious mind?" I asked, loath to discount this summary explanation once I saw F. W. weakening.

"How could it have been mine?" he answered. "I wasn't at the ouija-board."

I replied that perhaps the explanation lay in a combination of subconsciousness and telepathy. Perhaps the subconscious thoughts of F. W. had been transferred telepathically to Joan's subconsciousness or mine.

"Far-fetched!" exclaimed F. W. "Anyway, there were things spelled out there1 that weren't in my thought at all—the drunken driver, for instance. I never heard of him until to-night. If there ever was a drunken driver, he is probably dead by this time, and if he's dead the chances are that thought of his connection with my uncle's death is in the mind of nobody."

Joan and I, as we walked home from church the next morning, sifted the evidence offered by the communications F. W. had called forth. Several things were apparent.

For example, if I had held any lingering suspicion that Joan consciously pushed the tripod from letter to letter, or if she had suspected me, these doubts must disappear. With both of us blindfolded the spellings had proceeded practically unhampered. F. W.'s blindfold experiment had made the entire question of our mutual honesty pointless. At least, it demonstrated that there was no necessity for dishonesty.

Another fact stood out boldly. It is possible there was publicity given the death of Stephen L , especially in certain parts of the country. There was no special reason why the story should have been carried by the newspapers of the city in which Joan and I live, and I am quite sure it wasn't; yet, if news of Stephen's death was printed anywhere, there will be those inclined rather to believe that Joan or I read the item cursorily and forgot it, than that the fact of Stephen's existence and death should have come from out the nowhere to our ouija-board. But the Uncle Michael case was different.

Here was a farmer, killed in a remote community years ago. His obituary was printed in a country paper, with circulation limited to the immediate neighborhood. There isn't one chance in a million that Joan or I had ever heard of Uncle Michael.

This, then, stands out boldly: If the subconscious theory predicates a knowledge acquired normally, however completely the acquisition may have been forgotten by the conscious mind, it breaks down, in this instance at least. If for Uncle Michael to have been in our subconscious minds it was necessary that knowledge of him should have come to us in the past, whether near or distant, through the ordinary channels of the senses, then Uncle Michael simply was not in our subconscious minds.

I must anticipate my narrative. About three weeks after Uncle Michael appeared, F. W. called us up one evening and said he wanted to come and see us right away. He came, and brought with him this information: Uncle Michael had been extremely proficient at the mouth-organ and had been famous for his elderberry whistles.

"I swear to heavens," said F. W., "that when the ouija-board spelled those words they seemed to me the sheerest nonsense. I wrote the whole story to relatives back in the old home; and here's their answer; playing the mouth-organ and making elderberry whistles were real accomplishments with my Uncle Michael."

And thus was broken down the theory that perhaps Joan and I had simply been reading F. W.'s mind. Uncle Michael had told us facts, trivial facts, but true, that F. W. didn't know, any more than we did!

Let me close the Uncle Michael incident by quoting a paragraph from a letter F. W. wrote me recently from a hospital for American soldiers. The letter said:

"I was tremendously impressed by the exact detail of what I insist on calling Uncle Michael's recital and the communication of facts which no one of us was aware of at the time. The incident has come often to my thought, and always as a sort of convincing argument that we are, indeed, recipients of messages from afar."

VI

THE RECEIVING STATION

HE evidential character of the F. W. communications was, as F. W. has said, impressive. But I think Joan and I were even more impressed by the discovery that, while she and I could operate the ouija-board and likewise she and F. W., F. W. and I could not. This seemed to mean that Joan, not I, was the psychic.

We recalled what Stephen had said: "There is a psychic, a receiving station, here. She will remember having had the experience of feeling that someone was standing behind her and of turning to find nothing."

"Is that true, Joan?" I asked.

"Oh, I don't think so," she replied. "That's an experience every one has."

"Perhaps we are all of us psychic in some measure."

"Very kind of you to say so, Darby," she answered.

The truth is Joan was loath to acknowledge her psychic gift, especially loath to recognize that the communications came solely through her. Yet events subsequent to the F. W. messages have left her no escape from this conclusion. Even so, she has remained diffident. With the entire subject of psychic phenomena shrouded in uncertainty, her attitude is not to be wondered at.

Whether to avoid whatever of misunderstanding has attached itself to the words "psychic" and "medium," or whether simply to hold the fact in the case close to the ground, Stephen seldom uses the word "psychic," and never uses the word "medium." His term for one gifted as is Joan is "receiving station."

"What actually happens during the process of communication," says Stephen, "is more like the transmission of a wireless message than anything else in your experience. Our term receiving station is very good, not because it is metaphorical, but because it is the exact opposite of metaphorical."

Anticipating much of the experience this narrative relates, I digress here to trace the development of the receiving station that is Joan.

Stephen had been at work on the philosophy only a few weeks when I noted an odd thing.

Our method of taking down the ouija-board's words was this: As the pointer moved over the alphabet Joan would call out the letters, and we would both carry them in mind until a complete word was formed; at the end of a sentence I would remove my hands from the tripod and write it down.

After a while I noticed a tendency on Joan's part to call the letters before the tripod actually had picked them out.

"How do you do it, Joan?" I said. "You're ahead of the pointer."

"What do you mean?" she asked.

When I explained, she said: "I hadn't noticed it. Now that you speak of it, it's so. I do know sometimes what letter is coming next. But don't ask me how I know. I just do. The letters seem to pop into my thought."

Addressing Stephen, I said, "What is your method of communication?"

The conversation that followed is here reproduced practically in full, though at one turn it went somewhat afield. In answer to my question, Stephen spelled:

"I communicate by means of a medium quite material. I utilize a force which man does not now understand, but which in time he will. A few years ago men marveled at the ordinary telegraph; now they are reconciled to wireless."

"Do you mean," I asked, "that electricity operates this ouija-board?"

"But surely," Stephen replied, "though not electricity as you now understand it. The atomic force of which I speak might be called magnetic consciousness."

"Is there any other way besides this tiresome ouija-board method by which you could speak with us?" Joan asked.

"If you sat in a desert and looked toward the north," Stephen answered. "If you could make your minds clear."

"Explain," said I.

"Nirvana," said the ouija-board.

It was evident Stephen referred to the old Buddhistic practice whereby the worshiper seeks to free himself of all thought and desire, hoping thus to be absorbed into the ultimate.

"Is Nirvana, then, the goal toward which we're headed?" I asked.

"It is so called by some," Stephen answered. "The great fallacy of this religion, especially as interpreted by the Western World, is its doctrine of oblivion; yet it is among the wisest. True Nirvana is consciousness at its height."

Practicality is an outstanding feature of Joan's character. "I take no stock in Nirvana," she protested. "If you communicate with us through the medium of physical force, what I want to know is, why can't I see you?"

"Because your sense of color is not yet highly enough developed," the tripod spelled.

"Then, you seriously mean to say that you have a material body?" insisted Joan.

"But surely," said Stephen. "My present body has properties beyond your comprehension, such as color beyond the humanly visible spectrum."

"Have you sight, hearing, and the other human senses?" Joan asked.

"Consciousness on my plane has all of these, but not as you now know them," Stephen replied. "Do not misunderstand; consider my words—not as you now know them. I see as you see, and then some. For instance, I see matter in its component parts."

One night, a week or so after this conversation, Joan suddenly halted the tripod, sat silent a moment, then said: "Why, of all things! The idea of the letters is not only popping into my mind, but actually, Darby, I am beginning to see them, sometimes."

"See them? How do you mean you see them?"

"Just what I said," she answered. "I mean that every now and then I see a letter. Just before the tripod points it out I see it, sort of, in my mind. Understand?"

I was forced to admit I didn't.

A few more evenings and Joan's new experience had become clear-cut. Somehow, she said, she mentally visualized every letter, just prior to its being pointed out by the tripod. It would be well for Joan to describe the phenomenon in her own words. She says:

"The letters as they appeared in my mind were peculiarly characteristic. First, they were of distinct definition, just as the memory of a familiar object is distinctly defined in the mind's eye. In the second place, they were constituted of light, largely pink light, a sort of glow. The pink of the letters was surrounded by a fringe that began as a yellow, like the yellow of a coal flame, and shaded into a brilliant blue. The color-effect of the whole was not unlike that of a glowing bed of coals with flames spurting from the unburnt fuel around it.

"And the letters were of enormous size, much bigger than the immense type on a billboard. Toward the latter part of the experience they grew considerably smaller, though to the end they were very, very big.

"Each letter was visualized, not externally, but internally. The same effect of light visualized internally can be produced, I find, by pressing one's fingers strongly on the balls of the closed eyes. There will appear on the retina—at least so it was in my case—a rosy suffusion barred and crisscrossed by lines of yellow light, which, however, take no definite form.

"As to the manner in which the letters appeared: they sprang into being singly, at first with quite a space of time between; then they came closer together, but still singly. It was as though they were being shoved along a wire on which they had been strung, my line of vision being comprehensive of one letter only. Finally they began coming so fast that it was impossible for the ouija-board's tripod to keep pace with them.

"It was not necessary for me to close my eyes to see the letters; nor did their coming depend upon my concentrating my attention. I could think of other things, listen to Darby's questions, and when I wished ask a question myself.

"I have run the ouija-board only at infrequent intervals in the past year. As I dictate this statement to Darby, May 2,1919, I pause to attempt repetition of the experience of seeing the letters. The ouija-board runs, but as it did when the idea of the letters was just popping into my mind. I do not see the letters now."

The next step in Joan's psychic development caused our ouija-board to be temporarily abandoned. At best its operation was a physically tedious affair. And, too, as Joan has stated, the letters began to appear before her mental vision in such rapid succession that the tripod would sometimes be a whole word behind the letter Joan was announcing.

"Stephen," I said, finally, "if Joan sees these letters while sitting at the ouija-board, why couldn't she see them if she sat at a typewriter?"

"Let us make the experiment," replied Stephen, ever ready to try a new thing. "I do not know whether it will succeed. Joan, you sit at the typewriter, and, Darby, you stand behind her and place your hands on her temples."

We did as we were instructed, and after a wait of a minute or two Joan began to strike the keys of the typewriter, very deliberately. When a pause came, I pulled the paper out of the machine and asked Joan if she knew what had been written. She replied that she had only the haziest idea, that the letters came before her Vision, as usual, but that, because she was typing them down, she had made no effort to remember them. Here is what I found written on the paper:

this is slow kep at it we are al watching you this is fine i' should have answered your leter earlier the trouble here is that joan insists on puting the machine to its ordinary purposes the profesor is here and very much interested if this works out it means a wonderful method of comunication joan is doing fine she is making her mind frer than ever before undoubtedly this wil prove a great advance over the ouija board method

I have quoted the above just as it came— without capitals or punctuation and with only one letter employed in cases of double letters. The absence of any distinction between capitals and small letters had, of course, been characteristic of the ouija-board messages; the board carries only capital letters. I have already referred to the fact that it carries no punctuation marks, though by a system of pauses, which we soon learned, Stephen from the first did in a way indicate the punctuation. Again, as in the case of the typewriter, the ouija-board never troubled to double a letter.

Other than as the product of an engaging experiment the words written by the typewriter seemed of no importance. It proved later, however, that the part reading, "I should have answered your letter earlier; the trouble here is that Joan insists on putting the machine to its ordinary purposes," was most important.

We turned from the typewriter to the ouija board, and I asked Stephen if it would be possible for him to punctuate on the typewriter and use, where required, capitals and double letters. He said he could and would punctuate and capitalize, but that he simply wouldn't be bothered with double letters. Then we went to the typewriter again, and I started the thing off by asking, "Stephen, are you here?" The answer follows, written more rapidly than were the words of the first trial:

"I am here all right." (Supplying the double letters, I make good Stephen's abbreviated spelling.) "You need never be afraid of that when an experiment like this is going on. There are many others here too, many of very high degree."

"Could Joan and I communicate with those higher degrees?" I asked.

"You can communicate with any individual of degree higher than yourself, who is willing to make the effort to communicate with you. It is only individuals of a degree lower than your own that cannot communicate with you. But for the time stick with me."

"We shall, Stephen," I said. "But at least tell us about those high-degreed individuals who are so interested in this experiment."

And the answer was: "The whole kit and caboodle are here, greatly excited, and raising a very devil of a confusion. To tell you the truth, they all want to talk—and at once, as if they were only human. We carry our childhood with us, it seems. If Joan could speak German, French, and all the rest of the nonsensical human lingo—there should really be only one language—she would have to have ten dozen pairs of hands."

I asked Stephen why he didn't "bounce the kit and caboodle."

"Did you ever try to drive a pig through a hole in a fence?" was the answer.

Stephen then turned serious and requested that he might be allowed to continue his revelation, saying that the new method of communication would permit a much wider scope of discussion.

"But before we go on," he said, "there is something I would like to warn you about, especially Joan. Joan, you are the receiving station. As such you are of absolute importance to the delivery of the revelation I bring you two. But you are also a person of strong opinions. I ask you not to let your preconceived ideas and prejudices color my message. Keep your mind free, especially when I say something with which you do not altogether agree. Darby, you are the conceiving station. Remember that Joan could not communicate alone wholly successfully, nor could, I think, any one else. You can differ from me as much as you will; in fact, I rely on your questions to clarify the communication. But above all you must alleviate Joan's prejudices. You must prevent her own opinions coloring my words. And you must also be on the watch for a form of color that is likely to result, not simply from Joan's opinions, but from all that mass of thought and memory, her own experience, that lies dormant in her subconsciousness."

May I ask the reader to carry this speech in mind, along with those words: "I should have answered your letter earlier; the trouble here is that Joan insists on putting the machine to its ordinary uses"?

Many possibilities seemed to be opened up by the typewriter experiment. For one thing, it occurred to Joan and me that, if we were in receipt of genuine messages "from afar," they need not all be verbal. Why, for instance, could not musical ideas be communicated?

This thought interested us greatly, because, owing to the fact that Joan is not musical, a test was involved. I say Joan is not musical, even though as a child she received the sketchy sort of piano instruction that leaves a few bars of simple melody memorized and an ability mechanically to read a not too complicated score with something less than fifty per cent, accuracy. I am certain that Joan never has initiated a single musical idea.

I said to Stephen of the typewriter: "It has seemed to Joan and me that by use of the present method of communication Joan could sit at the piano, as she now sits at the typewriter, and produce music otherwise beyond her."

"I do not think so," Stephen wrote in reply. "Were Joan a musician, that would be possible. But she lacks both technic and tone-sense. You must understand that we can impress on the subconsciousness of a receiving station only those ideas that the station itself is capable of understanding. But let us make the effort. Joan, you sit at the piano. Darby, stand behind her and keep your hands on her temples. We shall see what happens."

The real value of this experiment, it proved, lay in making clear to Joan and me that, granted we were en rapport with a discarnate intelligence, there were limitations to the communication. Joan, herself incapable of originating Stephen's philosophy, could nonetheless grasp its conceptions. But to Joan a musical thought had no meaning, and therefore she could not successfully act as the medium of musical communication.

What happened, however, was interesting. Joan sat down at the piano. Suddenly her fingers began racing over the keyboard with a deftness unknown to them, and a series of great, crashing chords burst forth, harmonies suggestive of power, big organ-like effects that filled the room. But the chords were individual affairs, lacking continuity as a whole. Afterward Joan attempted to strike chords of equal complexity, but failed. It seemed that the harmonies she had produced as I stood with my hands on her temples were not in any ordinary sense of her own making. Stephen, too, disclaimed them, saying another than he had assisted from his side.

We employed the typewriter method for only a few evenings after the piano experiment. From the beginning Joan had complained that my pressing her temples resulted in headache. Finally the headaches became pronounced. We returned then to the ouija-board, but, as things turned out, not for long. It was Joan herself who suggested the likelihood of her being able simply to speak the letters, without their being either written on the typewriter or pointed out on the ouija-board.

"That would not have been possible a short time ago," spelled the tripod. "Let us try. I suggest, Darby, that during the experiment you hold Joan's wrists."

Just how my holding Joan's wrists might facilitate results I did not know. Nonetheless I did as Stephen advised. Instantly the experiment was a great success. With no mechanical handicap— tripod to follow or typewriter keys to strike—Joan was able to announce the letters with a fluency unmarred by confusion. The method seemed perfect, though its later development caused the early trials to appear tentative. There was but one difficulty; as both my hands were occupied, I could make no record. Yet Stephen asked that the experiment be continued over a period of two or three evenings.

On the third evening he said: "It is not necessary now for you to hold both wrists. Hold only one."

Two evenings later he said, "You need not hold her wrists at all."

I withdrew my hand, and the communication proceeded without interruption. At its close Stephen said: "Now touch her wrist. This will be your signal to Joan that the communication is over. Likewise, when the two of you seek communication, touch her wrist."

And so the ouija-board went behind the trunk in the closet—permanently. With much labor on Joan's part and mine, and, Stephen assured us, on his part also, the ouija-board, a toy accidentally thrown in our way, had laid the foundations of the Stephen philosophy. That a system of thought so suggestive should have come from two mere bits of wood seems to be a marvel exceeded only by the uniqueness of the philosophy itself.

Direct mental communication, which is Stephen's term, produced at first just letters, as had the ouija-board. Then one night Joan began to vary the letters by pronouncing now and then a word, and in the end the letters were discarded. For a while the words were pronounced slowly, with pauses between, and without variety of intonation. But soon they took on a fluency quite uncharacteristic of Joan's ordinary speech.

I do not mean to say that all communications received by the direct mental method have been equally fluent. When Joan is physically or mentally tired, the speech is slower and less certain. When a new personality— that is to say, purported personality—comes, one who has not spoken before through Joan, the speech is halting. When, of late, evidential matter has been sought,

63

involving names of persons or places or other identifying items of definiteness, there has been the appearance of great difficulty; the words come very slowly, with occasional corrections, and sometimes even the old spellings are reverted to. But in all other instances the communication possesses the ease of conversation, now and then assuming, as the communicator becomes animated, the flow of practised oratory.

I do not say that the voice that speaks is other than Joan's. I do say that the tone values are not hers. It is as though Joan were an accomplished mimic, imitating now Stephen, now the professor, or again one of the many other personalities that have come to us.

During the early attempts at mental communication Joan would sit absolutely immobile, other than for facial movements. In the course of half an hour an arm might cramp from being held too long in the same position. Stephen, not Joan, would ask me to move it. But gradually gestures came, gestures uncharacteristic of Joan, and so to the easy speech of accomplished acting there was added finally an equally mimic freedom of gesticulation.

But why marvel at the fluency of Joan's speech during the periods of communication or the freedom of her gestures? After all, it is only Joan that speaks. True and untrue. Assuredly it is none other than Joan who utters this word or that, whatever may be the source of the thought the word expresses. But the facility of expression is not the every-day Joan's. And there are other differences.

For one thing, during the periods of mental communication Joan speaks only occasionally in her own character. When she does it is to the personality whose thought she seems to be conveying. At Stephen's request she might in her own character describe a person or an object or a place, here or beyond. But never has she herself answered any question I have addressed to her personally. Always the answer comes from Stephen.

Again, after my touch has signaled the close of the communication, Joan has no memory of the communication itself or of any extraneous occurrence, such as the ringing of the telephone and my answering the call. And yet, despite this lack of memory, there is, during communication, no suggestion of unconsciousness. Joan is fully aware of all that happens, just as she was at the ouija-board. It seems simply that she holds herself aloof, permitting all outside of herself, whether on Stephen's side or her own and mine, to make as slight an impression on her every-day conscious mind as possible. She says:

"This holding of my thought vacant is a trick of the mind that I can scarcely explain. Stephen had said that mental communication would be possible if one could make his mind clear. At first this meant nothing to me. But during the typewriter experiments, when it was necessary no longer for me to announce the letters and help Darby piece them into words, I began to gain appreciation of what Stephen's 'clear mind' phrase meant. Then suddenly there came to me the knack of achieving the mental condition referred to. I rather think any one by practice could do the same; whether communication would necessarily result I, of course, do not know.

"Just what part Darby's touching of my wrist plays in the matter I have been unable to tell him. I know only that when he touches my wrist my mind clears—with some slight effort of my will—of thought and sense perception. When Darby again touches my wrist, thought and sense perception rush back.

"I have no memory of what happens in the interim, except that when Darby reads me his notes they sometimes sound familiar, like a thing I might have heard or read before."

To this sketch of Joan's psychic development there is to be added only the fact that now and then she has done what is called automatic writing. The first instance of this occurred a month or two after the mental method had been hit upon. She was sitting at her desk when suddenly her pencil broke off recording her own thoughts, and started to write instead what she recognized as a message. At first she resisted; then, being curious to see what the complete message might be, she permitted the pencil to have its own way. The communication was oddly interesting. It directed Joan to the solution of a little problem with which I had been struggling for days. Chief interest, however, lay in the fact that the suggested solution involved a something of which Joan at the time knew nothing, but the existence of which she later established. For personal reasons we withhold this message.

And now, is Joan's psychic gift abnormal, or, as I have thought, supernormal?

Stephen says: "It is misunderstanding that causes one to regard Joan's experience as either abnormal or supernormal. It is, in fact, simply normal, just as any special talent—that, for instance, of the artist—is normal, though unpossessed by the great majority."

VII

TRIVIALITIES

WITH the tedious ouija-board abandoned Joan and I soon lost what slender interest we had in tests and evidence. Before the advent of direct mental communication we were knee-deep in Stephen's philosophy; now we found ourselves immersed in it, so absorbed that the question of who or what Stephen might be seemed to us more and more definitely a pointless query. Here was being offered a new argument for the survival of personality after death. The terms of that argument made it possible for us reasonably to conceive Stephen as a personality that had survived death. The reasonableness of this conception might not be conclusive. But was it not of greater evidential worth than all the testings we might contrive?

Compared with Stephen's philosophy, how trivial the evidential messages seemed! Stephen's identification of himself had not been trivial. But that bit of evidence had come to us unsought. We had not sought the Uncle Michael tests; even so, his method of making himself known to F. W. had seemed rather trashy. Why had he not spoken out plainly, giving the simple facts? Why, instead of saying, "I am your Uncle Michael," had he chosen to ejaculate, "Mouth-organ," and followed it up with "Elderberry whistle"? The Fred Q. test we had sought, to the extent that I had asked to speak with some one I knew in this life; surely the identification data offered by Fred Q. were trivial enough. "Gunboats!" The more one sought evidence the more trivial were the messages received.

Our decision that tests led nowhere was reached during the brief period between the typewriter experiment and the first mental communication; that is, on one of the last evenings we spent at the ouija-board. On this evening I told Stephen I wanted to talk with some one other than himself, some one of whom I knew nothing, but who could give me facts that later I might verify.

"Testing, always testing!" spelled Stephen, in disgust.

The tripod lay idle awhile, then began to move with an annoying uncertainty.

"Armand Dupont," it spelled, after many tentative moments.

"And who are you?" I asked.

For two or three minutes the pointer oscillated from one side of the board to the other and finally spelled, with difficulty, the following:

"I was an artist, a Frenchman. I was killed at Ypres."

Joan knows no French. I said to Armand, "If you are a Frenchman, tell me what the French word for child is."

I had expected Armand, if he answered at all, to spell "enfant." Instead the tripod spelled "bebe," a word belonging to my reading, not my thinking, vocabulary. Whether this French word had somehow been assimilated by Joan she cannot say; she believes it not impossible. Therefore, there is probably nothing evidential in Armand's answer, though at the time it impressed us.

I cannot explain the uneasiness that possessed Joan and me during the brief conversation Armand and I had carried on. The uncanny, by this time, had disappeared from our meetings with Stephen and the professor. Yet Armand somehow was ghostly.

Stephen came. We were heartily glad to have him back. Without reference to Armand, he plunged into philosophic byways, and before long Joan and I had forgotten all about the terrifying Frenchman. Stephen talked for almost an hour, when of a sudden the tripod wabbled and again spelled, "Armand Dupont," following the name up with this, "The Marne was once my home."

"We don't want to talk with you," said Joan.

"But I want to talk," answered Armand. "I was an artist in Paris. My picture, top floor, Rue de la Chapelle. My studio was there with Jack."

Then there was an incoherent spelling or two; and then came Stephen again. Again we welcomed him; Armand in his second appearance had proved more uncanny than in his first.

"What about Armand?" I said.

"You mustn't mind him," Stephen replied. "His body was blown into a million pieces. The shock lost him a part of his intelligence. He will be all right in a short time. You wanted a test; you have had it. Write and find out if there ever was an Armand Dupont."

We did no such thing. Instead, Joan and I agreed then and there that Stephen's philosophy was, as the professor had said, its own best test. Granted we instituted inquiry and found that Armand Dupont had in truth been killed at Ypres, that "Jack" was his friend, etc., would we not immediately be confronted with puzzling questions regarding the subconscious mind, telepathy, and what-not? Premeditated testings resulted only in "mouth organs" and "stolen shirts" and in uncanny things like the coming to our ouija-board of a personality that had "lost part of his intelligence."

"Tests that are worth while," I said to Joan, "must come unsought!"

"And even then," she answered, "one can always find some plausible theory by which they can be explained away. Also, one test creates an appetite for another. The thing becomes an endless search."

It required, then, only the development of direct mental communication, and the wide philosophic interest it stimulated, to drive all wish for evidential messages from us.

At the time, I should add, Joan and I did not realize that grief for a dear, vanished friend causes men and women to long for little personal manifestations of the friend's continued life. We did not realize that in such a case the trivial message is often the most convincing. Joan and I, while not young, are youngish. Dear friends have left us, my father and mother and Joan's father. But up to this time we had not wished to talk with them; the thought repelled us. I used to wonder why. The reason was, I think, that, profoundly impressed as we were with Stephen's philosophy, we did not really believe in Stephen himself. Even so, I know now we would have cried out for communication with our dead, if memory of them had been gripping our emotions as memory of the dead husband grips the wife left here to plod the road alone. Joan and I, impersonal in our contact with Stephen and the others, were mere students of philosophy.

Rapidly Stephen's philosophy took final form. On the foundations the ouija-board had laid with slow laboriousness mental communication quickly built the superstructure. Thereafter the philosophy's ramifications were more thoroughly explored, doubtful points were cleared, qualifications were made. And then, because with the philosophy an accomplished fact, there seemed little left for discussion, Stephen was sought less frequently. When he did come, or when others came, the war— America by this time had cast her lot in—was the insistent topic. Occasionally Stephen would ask me when I intended to set about telling others that which he had revealed (his word) to me, but there was no urging—just a quiet reminder that some report was called for.

Thus the experience I relate, which began December 7,1916, reached the date of January 22, 1919.

VIII

FRED Q. AGAIN

ON the afternoon of January 22,1 1919, Joan went shopping. Toward dinnertime I picked her up, and as we drove homeward she told me she had purchased a book, lately published, called *The Seven Purposes*, a record of psychic communications received by Margaret Cameron. "Who's Margaret Cameron?" I asked. "All I know about Margaret Cameron," Joan answered, "is that she writes short stories for the magazines. I've read a number of them."

"What's the book like?" I asked.

"It's subtitled 'An Experience in Psychic Phenomena,'" was Joan's reply. "I didn't take time to look through it. We'll try reading it aloud after dinner."

By eight o'clock we were settled, Joan at one side of the reading-table and I at the other, with an electric lamp of two forty-watt bulbs between us. In addition, a wall lamp was burning. Every corner of the room was well lighted. I unwrapped *The Seven Purposes*. Joan said she would read a chapter and I the next. She read to the fifth line from the bottom of the second page of the introduction then stopped, an exclamation on her lips.

Briefly, what she had read was a statement by the author of *The Seven Purposes* that twenty-five years prior to the experiences related in her book she had found amusing possibilities in a planchette, had "played" with it, "like other young persons," at intervals, for several years, but had regarded the assumption that the planchette's assertions emanated from disembodied personalities as rather absurd. Next she told how some time in 1917 she had been influenced by the war's revival of psychical interest to buy a planchette, how for close to a year it remained untouched in its box, how then she made an unsuccessful effort to operate it, and how finally, two weeks later, two friends of hers—a Mrs. Wylie and a Miss Gaylord, sisters—had told her they had been trying "to get into touch with their brother Frederick."

I now quote an entire sentence from the book:

A day or two later we [Frederick's sisters and Margaret Cameron] tried planchette together, with some success. It moved briskly, wrote, "Frederick . . . mother . . . love . . . happy . . ." and other detached words.

Joan, reading the above sentence aloud, reached the word "Frederick," then stopped abruptly. She raised her eyes from the page and, with a surprised look, glanced across the room, then exclaimed:

"Why, this is Fred Q.'s book!"

"You mean the Frederick *The Seven Purposes* mentions is our Fred Q.? That's a weird notion. What makes you think so?"

"I just saw Fred Q. standing there, at my desk, and he told me," she answered.

"Saw him!" I said, staring into the empty air in front of Joan's desk. "How did he tell you? Did he speak to you?"

"I don't think so. At least I heard nothing. But he told me just the same."

When she regained her composure, Joan added: "As I reached the name 'Frederick' something prompted me to raise my eyes. I did so, and saw Fred Q. I wasn't frightened. The thing became startling only when it was all over and I began telling you about it. Fred Q. was standing by the end of the desk with the dark mahogany of the closet door as a background. I knew him instantly. He looked perfectly natural, save that there was a brilliancy about him. His face shone. His head was bent a little to one side, and down a bit. He looked at me sort of from under his brows, with quizzical, half-mischievous eyes. His mouth smiled."

I was struck by Joan's description of a pose characteristic of Fred Q. She had known him but slightly.

Fred Q., he who had helped himself to my shirts, was the best man at Joan's and my wedding. Before that splendid occasion Joan had met him only once. Shortly after Joan and I were married he spent a Sunday afternoon in our home. Following that afternoon the meetings of Joan and Fred Q. had been limited to chance encounters. From late in 1910 to 1915, when he died, Joan did not exchange with him two-score words.

My own conversations with Fred Q. from 1910 on were almost as meager as Joan's. Our ways drifted so far apart that, though I knew of his illness, I did not realize its seriousness. Indeed, I had taken his recovery for granted, and was, therefore, greatly shocked when I learned of his death. Then gradually he passed from my mind, so that when in 1917 I had asked to talk with some departed soul I had known here, and Fred Q. came, I was surprised. Why Fred Q.? There were others gone on whom I had known quite as well, He had served me faithfully the night Joan and I were married, but, after all, this was the result of circumstances rather than long acquaintance.

Joan and I did not go on with our out-loud reading of *The Seven Purposes*. A bit upset, she turned to a magazine, leaving me to examine the book alone.

The author of *The Seven Purposes* had been most careful, I found, not to identify Frederick Gaylord; the name "Frederick Gaylord" was fictitious. I found, though, as I read on in the book, circumstances that might be regarded as pointing to our Fred Q., yet nothing definite. On the other hand, I found references that were meaningless to me, details concerning Frederick Gaylord's home associations that might have been true of Fred Q.; if so, I knew nothing of them. I did not, for example, know in what city, or even in what part of the country, his parents lived. Indeed, some of the more personal detail was contradictory to what I thought I knew relative to Fred Q.'s family.

If my own knowledge of Fred Q.'s connections was limited, Joan's was zero. But, for that matter, she could have known much, and the fact would have remained that, after reading less than two pages of *The Seven Purposes*, offering no hint of the identity of Frederick Gaylord except that he had two sisters, one married and one single, she had announced:

"This is Fred Q.'s book."

But was it?

The next day Joan wrote to Margaret Cameron—in care of her publishers, for want of a better address. Joan stated she had received a communication that asserted Frederick Gaylord was So-and-so; she begged to know if such was really the case. The letter was not mailed until the day following; we debated seriously whether to send it at all.

On January 31st Joan received a reply from Margaret Cameron, beginning as follows:

Your interesting, not to say startling, letter reached me last night . . . and I wish you would tell me more about your experience with Fred Q. From one of his sisters I have obtained permission to tell you that your Fred Q. is the man whose communication forms rather a large part of "The Seven Purposes."

And so once more, after months of limiting our interest in Stephen to his philosophy, Joan and I were bowled over by so-called evidence. We suffered something of the same shock we underwent when we discovered that Stephen of the ouija-board had told the true story of Stephen L .

"Darby," said Joan, "you know more about the verbal messages we have had than I. Though they come through me, I understand nothing, really, of the part I play in their transmission. Whatever conviction they carry to me rests on ground similar to that of your own conviction. But this vision of Fred Q. is different. It was something I saw, outside of me, just as I now see you."

Is there any light thrown on Joan's vision—her first and only experience of the sort—by the subconscious-mind theory, by telepathy and the rest?

Personally I am convinced that Joan did, as a matter of fact, see an external something resembling Fred Q. This experience, as she says, is different. Manifestly telepathy did not cause that vision. Joan's subconscious mind may have—but how, by what manner of thought projection?

And this speaking of Frederick Gaylord's correct name—was it the result of mere guess? The two pages of *The Seven Purposes* that Joan had read gave no data that would have aided the guess. Joan did not know Margaret Cameron or any one knowing her. Could guess be the solution of the mystery? If so, how did it happen that simultaneously with Joan's making the guess she saw Fred Q.? Hallucination? But why was the guess accompanied by the hallucination?

If the occurrence had been of an isolated character, if Joan never before had received a purported communication from the dead, I for one, in attempting to answer these questions, would have refused to consider the spiritistic explanation, however impossible non-spiritistic explanations might appear. But the occurrence was backgrounded in the remarkable coming and identification of Stephen, the marvel of his philosophy, the piquing F. W. communications. With such a background the incident of *The Seven Purposes* could not be dismissed without full recognition of at least the possibility that the phenomenon involved was not other than it purported to be. Surely this recognition is necessary in the light of events the incident precipitated.

Margaret Cameron, in replying to Joan's letter, had gone on to say: "I hope you will give me permission to show your letter to Mrs. K—, a friend of mine, who, having lost her husband, is keenly desirous of obtaining some definite proof that identity continues after what we call death. I think this incident might be of help and comfort to her."

The woman who had lost her husband! It had never occurred to Joan and me that this old, euphemistic phrase, "lost her husband," might carry a wholly literal meaning. What has been lost can be found!

But before taking up the messages that, later on, came through Joan for Mrs. K., I shall detail Stephen's statement of the facts of "coloring." Otherwise much of the interest of the Mrs. K. communications would be lost.

IX

Coloring

STEPHEN grounds the reality of communication in the subconscious mind—that of the receiving station. He states that by means of a physical force, now unknown to men, he is able to transfer his thought to the subconscious Joan. But mere transference of Stephen's thought to Joan's subconsciousness is not sufficient for the purpose of actual communication. The message must be lifted out of Joan's subliminal into her conscious mind, or that of some other person.

It will be seen, then, that successful communication depends not wholly on the degree of accuracy with which Joan's subconscious mind registers the thought Stephen seeks to convey. It depends also on the degree of accuracy with which that thought passes out of Joan's subconsciousness into consciousness —Joan's own consciousness in the case of automatic writing, mine in the case of direct mental communication, hers and mine jointly in the case of the ouija-board.

Says Stephen, speaking particularly of ouija-board communications: "Coloring results when the conscious mind of the receiving station overrules the subconscious. Suppose I started to give you a name. 'M-a-r,' I spell. By the time I get that far Joan's conscious mind may have supplied the letter 'y,' because one who is with her much is named Mary. Now, the name I tried to give might have been Martha, Marion, Marie, Maria, Marietta."

There you have what Stephen calls coloring in its simplest form. How complicated its possibilities are can be appreciated when one considers that all of a person's past thoughts and perceptions are stored away in his subconsciousness. Can a receiving station's subconscious thoughts and memories overrule a message?

You will remember that embedded in the first message received at the typewriter was this: "I should have answered your letter earlier." These words had no bearing on the rest of the message, except as Stephen added: "The trouble here is that Joan insists on putting the machine to its ordinary purposes." Joan, in fact, had neglected to answer a letter that called for an early reply, and her neglect was on her conscience. She types practically all of her correspondence. Consequently the act of sitting at the typewriter called up unconscious remembrance of the unanswered letter, and that memory, wholly unrelated to Stephen or the thought he was seeking to convey, wrote itself, involuntarily so far as the conscious Joan was concerned, on what I might call Stephen's typewriter.

Says Stephen: "It is impossible for me to get a message through Joan or through any other receiving station without combating hundreds of such subconscious memories."

You will recollect that the first words Uncle Michael spelled on the ouija-board spoke of a country road, a cold day, of his taking F. W. to meet his mother, and of two teams. F. W. said he remembered no such experience. Moreover, the message was rather incoherent; we thought it

80

strange that two teams were required to carry F. W. And yet it was on a country road that Uncle Michael met his death, and the day was cold. And two teams did figure in Uncle Michael's later message—his own and the drunken driver's.

The message concerning the drunken driver might be beyond verification; nonetheless, it was intelligible. The two teams, first appearing in an illogical connection, finally placed themselves in one that was quite coherent.

The inaccuracy of Uncle Michael's initial message, it would seem, was the result of coloring. Joan, as a small child, had many a time been driven over a country road on cold days, to a railroad station, there to meet her mother. Uncle Michael, attempting to convey a message relative to his death on a country road, awakened in Joan memory of her own experience, and that memory blended itself with the thought F. W.'s uncle was seeking to communicate; so that all he got through was the suggestion of the country road and the cold day and the anomaly of the two teams. And if the communication had ended there, no message of meaning would have been conveyed to F. W.

"Coloring," Stephen elaborates, "occurs not only as the result of the receiving station's conscious mind overruling the subconscious, but also whenever, in the course of communication, the subconscious mind frees itself from our control. Immediately it gives expression to that which is its own thought and experience. In the case of the ouija-board there is the additional possibility of conscious overruling. Of this there is not so much danger in direct mental communication, because the conscious mind is more dormant. There is grave danger, however, of subconscious coloring."

It was the professor who said one evening, communicating mentally: "I shall demonstrate to you, my dear sir, the action of the subconscious mind. You recognize, of course, that at this minute Joan is exercising a minimum of control over her mental processes. I shall now lift the control that we here have been exercising. First, you speak a word— any word."

I spoke the first word that occurred to me— horse.

Immediately Joan began to talk quite in her own character, though disjointedly. She said: "My saddle turned—street-car—in front, of the hospital—Hobson—George—picnic."

And so the words kept coming, most of them carrying no meaning to me.

"Come back, professor!" I said. "This is nonsense."

In a minute or two the professor again spoke. He said: "Of course, it's nonsense to you, but not to Joan. She was giving expression to memories of her past, one memory linking itself with another. Now touch her wrist and ask her what she meant."

Joan took the paper on which I had written the words, read them, and smiled.

"Why," said she, "here I have been telling you about the time my saddle-horse took fright at a street-car—long before I knew you, Darby. The girth slipped. Yes, it was in front of a hospital."

"Did it have anything to do with a picnic?" I asked.

"No, but George did. George took me to the picnic, and Hobson, my dog, insisted on following us, and George had to chase him back."

"Could Hobson be the link between George and the accident?" I asked.

"Why, of course," Joan answered. "Hobson was trailing along the day my saddle turned, and was very much excited over the spill. But what's the point of all this?"

After explaining the professor's experiment, I again touched Joan's wrist. The professor reappeared, saying:

"I think you now understand what Stephen means when he tells you that in communicating through Joan he must combat the entire of her subconsciousness, even though it is the very instrument of his communication. Let us suppose he wanted to communicate a message concerning a man named Hobson. If he were not in perfect control of Joan's mental processes, it is apparent that that word 'Hobson' might awaken in Joan such a chain of subconscious memories that her subliminal would free itself from Stephen's control and she would start garrulously relating the story of her accident and such other memories as the turned saddle suggested. In such an instance Stephen's message would be mixed up with the outcroppings of Joan's subliminal; the communication would be inaccurate, or even incoherent, or the message might be completely blocked."

Stephen says: "It is very hard to get a name through, that of a person or a place. Dates are very hard, and so are all other concrete items. It is a small matter for me to convey through this station an idea that impinges on no association personal to the station. I can dictate my revelation through Joan, unfamiliar as its terms have been to her, with much greater accuracy than I could state through her my old preference in furniture or flowers. Mention by me of any of the little familiar things of living would stir immediately a host of her own subconscious associations."

Thus warned by Stephen and the professor, and by my own observations, I have scanned closely all communications for outcroppings from Joan's subliminal store. Scarcely a trace of such have I found in the philosophical communications; Joan approached the philosophy without metaphysical thought of her own, and in all matters of practical judgment she has sought, during moments of actual communication, to suppress her own opinions, even as Stephen of the typewriter requested. But evidential messages, which in the nature of things are largely personal, have showed at times the mark of Joan's subliminal. Sometimes I note the coloring; quite as frequently Joan, in reading my notes, spots it, she alone being able to detect shades that result from the minutiae of her experience.

One more word should be added. I quote Stephen:

"Sometimes we utilize a subconscious memory to suggest a word or idea that otherwise we might not be able to get through. The subconscious Joan is very much alive to the danger of coloring. This causes her to resist test messages. We can sometimes break her resistance down by suggesting a memory of her own and, in a roundabout fashion, working from that memory to the idea we are seeking to put through. Thus we take her off her guard."

Concluding this outline of Stephen's statement of the purported facts of coloring, may I express my conviction that the true worth of any evidential communication, as, for instance, the message that undertakes to give personal facts concerning the earth-life of one who has gone on, can be estimated not on the basis of whether the entire communication is accurate? If in the midst of a hundred inaccuracies one thing accurate is found, something that cannot reasonably be attributed to the receiving station's own knowledge, conscious or subconscious, one has a measure of proof of—

Of what? Of telepathy? Of survival of the dead? Of what?

X

FROM A RESEARCH VIEWPOINT

IT was the woman who was searching for her lost husband that finally awakened in Joan and me appreciation of what evidential tests mean to the researchers.

Margaret Cameron had written Mrs. K. and told her how Joan, upon reading less than two pages of *The Seven Purposes*, had spoken Frederick Gaylord's true name. Thereupon Mrs. K. wrote Joan. Commenting first on the evidential importance of the Fred Q. incident, and then speaking of her interest in psychical research, Mrs. K. said:

"At first, I suppose, I had no belief in survival; it was to me an unthinkable hypothesis. But little by little I have built up, like a coral insect, a reef of hope—just grains of evidence, mounting and mounting, until sometimes for a moment the reef shows above the dark waters. . . . Then the waters close over again and the reef is hidden. But still I hunt for proof—to build my reef quite up into the sunshine."

Mrs. K., on the death of her husband, had plunged into study of psychical research; then, as she phrased it, she began "knocking at doors." Thus, unacquainted with Margaret Cameron, she had, upon reading *The Seven Purposes*, put herself in touch with its author. So, too, she rapped now at Joan's door. In answering her knock, Joan and I did not set ourselves the task of convincing her that her husband really had survived death. We would simply lay our facts before her.

For all her hope, Mrs. K. was, we were to find, strongly under the influence of those theories which, while they admit the genuineness of psychic phenomena, seek to explain them on some non-spiritistic basis—subconsciousness, telepathy, and that most speculative, yet to the modern scientific mind enticing, abstraction, cosmic consciousness. Cosmic consciousness—the vast reservoir of the whole, in which, it has been conceived, all personal experience survives, not as such, but as part of the impersonal life of the universe!

Only the motive of Mrs. K.'s search was emotional; the manner of its conduct was the reverse. No communication, so called, would be accepted by her as emanating from the dead until such time as she had definitely failed to explain it on some other basis. Evidence was the biggest word in her vocabulary, just as it had been the smallest in Joan's and mine.

Mrs. K.'s letter requested that we send her any messages we received that might even by remote chance be intended for her. We agreed to do so. No word, though, had ever been intrusted to us for third persons, not even for friends. There seemed little likelihood that we would be asked to deliver a message to a woman we had never seen, one whom several hundred miles separated from us.

Joan, in replying to Mrs. K.'s letter, took the position that all tests could be explained away, even the vision of Fred Q. Hallucination, one might say; and there, in a way, was an end to the vision's evidence! She told Mrs. K. of the existence of

Stephen's philosophy, and ventured the opinion that the case for survival likely to prove most acceptable to present-day men and women would be found in some such statement of survival's reasonableness.

"We must hope to be fortified," wrote Joan, "not only with evidential tests, but with conclusions any man can reach once he has grasped the premises."

I quote now at some length from a letter Mrs. K. wrote Joan on March 8, 1919, controverting this idea of ours and insisting there must be tests before there can be proof.

"Suppose," said Mrs. K., "Darby is called up some day on the long-distance telephone, and the telephone operator says, 'South America wants to speak to you, Darby—top of the Andes.'"

"Darby, surprised, says, 'Well, who on earth wants to speak to me from the top of the Andes?'

"'John Smith,' answers the telephone operator. 'He says he has a message from God for you.'

"Darby says: 'A message from God? John Smith? But John Smith disappeared ten years ago!'

"The telephone operator replies, 'Maybe he did, but he's here on the line now, and he has a message for you from the Eternal.'

"Darby, listening in the receiver, says, 'Hello!' And a voice comes through, saying: '.Hello, Darby! I've got a message from God for you!'

"To which Darby, very much startled, replies: 'But hold on! Who are you?'

"'Why, I'm John Smith, and I'm going to give you a message from God: He says—'

"'Hold on, hold on! How do I know you are John Smith? I don't recognize your voice.'

"'Well, I am. Now listen to what I am going to say. God says—'

"'Yes, but how do I know you are John Smith?'

"'Oh, confound you! Because—because— well, don't you remember walking down Fifth Avenue with me, and we stopped at Forty Second Street, and my umbrella blew wrong side out?'

"'Oh, Lord, yes! Of course! John Smith! Well, well, well! Awfully glad to hear your voice. Where have you been all this time? Go ahead, John. What have you got to say from God?'

"Now the umbrella," Mrs. K. continued, "is, I admit, frivolous. But it authenticates the whole message from the top of the Andes."

It does, certainly. Still, if John Smith's message from God, once listened to, proved of such a nature that it must be true in view of one's already possessed knowledge, John Smith's identification would have been unnecessary. The message would be the important thing, and not whether it really was John Smith who delivered it.

Yet Mrs. K.'s little fiction could not be simply waved aside. It represented at least a viewpoint; hers, and that, doubtless, of many others.

Then, too, Mrs. K. was groping out in the darkness, not for a principle, but for a familiar hand. By comparison Joan and I were of the academy. To Mrs. K. the personal, even the trivial, if characteristic of him whom she sought, meant more than any principle—provided, of course, knowledge of the triviality could not possibly have been in the receiving station's own mind. . . .

A strange thing had happened, strange to Joan and me. For months Stephen's communications, and those of the others with whom we were accustomed to talk, had been most fluent. Not often did we seek communication, but when we did the words came with easy naturalness. And for months no personality new to us had appeared.

Then, without warning, the words of Stephen were broken in on one night—shortly after receipt of Mrs. K.'s first letter—by one whom I did not recognize. The really curious thing was that the new personality spoke no actual words; instead, the long-abandoned practice of spelling was revived. The few letters that came seemed meaningless.

The first letters spelled were "d-a-v-i." Then, after a pause, came the single letter "f." Then the combination was repeated, except that for the "i" there was substituted a "y."

Could these letters, puzzling to Joan and me, be intended for Mrs. K.?

An evening or two later two words, or what seemed to be two words, were spoken, very uncertainly. They were repeated several times, sometimes one word being spoken first, sometimes the other. They were "mack" and "port."

In sending these words and the letters to Mrs. K., Joan wrote: "I do not know whether they will mean anything to you; certainly they mean nothing to Darby and me."

Imagine our interest when, in a few days, Joan received a letter from Mrs. K. stating that her husband's first name and middle initial had been David F., and that their summer home had been in a little town called Mackeysport. Neither "David F." nor "Mackeysport" had come through accurately, though there was no mistaking the connection between them and the letters and syllables the unknown communicator had spoken. Joan and I had not known the name of Mrs. K.'s husband or that of the town in which the K.'s had had their summer home. Mrs. K.'s correspondence did not question the sincerity of our ignorance. Yet here again was the old question as to what Joan does and does not know subconsciously. Mrs. K. wrote Joan:

"You say you have read things I have written. Some of them were dedicated to my husband, 'David F.' Also the word 'Mackeysport' appears in some of these dedications. Now, of course, if your eye should have fallen on these words, 'David F.' and 'Mackeysport,' you would not have remembered them one minute afterward. But somewhere in your subliminal they remained; and they might have emerged in communication. ... If you had never read anything I had written, then the evidence of d-a-v-i f would have been most important."

There was no refuting this argument. Joan had read certain of Mrs. K.'s writings. Therefore, she might have seen the name of Mrs. K.'s husband and that of the summer-home town.

In the mean time four more letters had interrupted Stephen, apparently delivered by the same unknown. They were repeated over and over again, as though being greatly insisted on. They were "m-d-s-e." It was evident these letters might be an abbreviation of the word "merchandise." We forwarded them to Mrs. K.

"The appearance of 'm-d-s-e' is interesting," Mrs. K. wrote in reply, "because my husband was a merchant. But that, too, must be somewhat discounted by the fact that Darby's is a related profession, and it is not impossible —though it is to a very high degree improbable—that he has noticed references, which used to appear more or less frequently in trade journals, to Mr. K.'s business."

To this Joan replied as follows: "To be outspoken, Darby and I don't agree with you about 'm-d-s-e.' As a matter of pure rationality we are

91

willing to grant all you have said relative to 'd-a-v-i' and 'Mack-port.' The 'm-d-s-e' affair, however, is another matter. While both Darby and I are connected with the same general calling as that which was followed by your husband, ours is a wholly different branch of the work. There is not one chance in a thousand that we ever heard of your husband as a merchant."

In fact, Joan and I had known nothing whatever concerning Mrs. K.'s family relations. Up to the time Margaret Cameron wrote to us about her, she was a mere name, and the name bore no clue as to whether she was a married woman. And need I add that during the entire period of the Mrs. K. communications Joan and I refrained scrupulously from seeking any detail of her personal life?

Another strange thing now happened. On only rare occasions had Joan written automatically. One afternoon, as we sat discussing a matter wholly unrelated to psychical concerns, Joan said of a sudden, "Give me a pencil, quick!" I handed her a pencil, and on the back of a magazine, which she picked up from the table, she began hurriedly to scribble. When she had finished, she said, "I had a feeling that some one wanted to give a message and that I could write it down."

With difficulty I deciphered what she had written over the magazine's printed matter and pictures. It follows:

There is a cottage in the midst of a garden. A sandy road. There are tall flowers. A path among the flower beds to the barn. A woman sat in the barn.

On receipt of a copy of this communication Mrs. K. wrote that it was without meaning to her.

It seemed later, however, that there was very definite meaning in it—for Mrs. K.

Before Mrs. K. had had time to write Joan that the message meant nothing, it was repeated in mental communication, being accompanied by an attempt to revise it. But much confusion resulted. Clear reference, however, was made to an "upper window that overlooked the garden between the cliffs, at which you used to sit and write," though there was apparent dissatisfaction with the word "cliffs." The attempt at revision seemed so unsuccessful that we put off sending Mrs. K. the additional matter.

The same evening the revision of the "woman who sat in a barn" message was attempted the following was received:

"Dormer window. No." [By which apparently was meant that the window in question was not a dormer window.) "She" (meaning Joan) "has never seen a big window such as this, and has not the word to describe it."

Mrs. K.'s comment was, "'Dormer window' has no real significance for me; and yet I find myself unwilling to let go of it, because Mr. K. was obsessed by building large windows."

The next message that came, a few nights later, was rather incoherent. Concerning it, Joan made to Mrs. K. the following report:

"There was apparently an effort on the part of some one, we don't know who, to give a message about a boat with bright-colored sails. The word 'yellow' came, then the word 'no,' then the word 'yellow' again, leaving Darby in doubt as to the entire message. The word 'Venice' also came, but it, too, was followed by 'no.'"

This impressed Mrs. K. apparently so little that her letters neglected to comment on it.

There came, about a week later, still another message which we felt might be intended for Mrs. K. It was in part as follows:

"Dear: This is just a note to tell you that I am quite well and happy. My only wish for you is to be happy and content, too. I wish you would think of me as having gone on to prepare a place for you. And yet I have not gone from you, because, though you cannot see me, I can see you. ... Don't grieve so. The image of my hand that you see is not half so real as the hand I lay on your hair, that you don't see. ... I love you, dearest."

I confess that the communication which says, "I am happy" and "I am with you," leaves me unimpressed. This particular communication failed to interest Mrs. K. She wrote, "The message might be from 'any husband to any wife.'" And yet embedded in it there proved to be a sentence of strikingly evidential quality.

Up to this point, with messages scattered over the latter part of February, 1919, and the early days of March, nothing seemed to have been accomplished. "D-a-v-i" and "Mackport" were ruled out. "M-d-s-e" was in dispute; nothing was to be gained by insisting on its evidential worth. None of the other messages seemed to carry meaning, except that concerning the dormer window, which wasn't a dormer window; and here the evidential possibility was slight, consisting of the mere fact that Mr. K. had been obsessed of building big windows.

And then a new series of messages began.

Before leaving the communications already mentioned, I shall ask the reader to fix in mind the last four, which for the sake of convenience can be labeled in this wise: The "woman who sat in the barn" message, including the attempted revision;

the "big window" message; the "yellow sail" message, and the message of "any husband to any wife."

XI

AN OBSCURITY MADE CLEAR

WITH one exception the Mrs. K. messages thus far received had been communicated mentally; the new series came by the way of automatic writing. On March 11th, Joan, in my absence, put pencil to paper with the thought that some further word of interest to Mrs. K. might come. I quote the proceedings that ensued, the communications themselves being indicated by the word "pencil":

Pencil (writing after Joan had sat waiting for ten minutes): Do you remember the necktie with the scrawly pattern? [These words were followed by great indecision on the part of the pencil. Then the writing was continued, but apparently by another communicator.]

Pencil: He wants to say he never liked to wear it. Joan: Who is this? Pencil: Charles—Charles—Charles.

Joan: Do you know Mrs. K.?

Pencil: Yes, very well. Good friends with her and—

Joan: Are you trying to say "her husband"?

Pencil: Yes, yes. Wading in a brook, wading in a brook—no, brooks.

Joan: Is this Charles talking?

Pencil: Yes, but not my necktie—not my necktie.

Joan: All right, Charles. It's not your necktie. But did you go wading in a brook? Pencil: No.

Joan: Did you know Mrs. K. when she was a little girl? [Joan thought that possibly Charles was a childhood friend of Mrs. K. and that they might have gone wading together as children.]

Pencil: No. [And then the pencil came to a halt, writing nothing more for a space of seventeen minutes. Then—]

Pencil: Charles wading in brooks. [Again the pencil stopped; whereupon Joan spoke the name of Stephen, asking him to come and straighten matters out.]

Pencil (apparently Stephen): Be patient. The words are not for you. [And again the pencil was idle for a while.]

Pencil (not Charles, but evidently the original communicator, who Joan had thought might be Mr. K.): Necktie — did not like.

She will remember the incident. She said I was fussy.1 My friend Charles is here with me. My hand—my hand—my hand. [I italicize the last words; they proved very interesting.]

Joan: Can you give some other identification in addition to "necktie"?

Pencil: Beside the lake, beneath the trees, laughing and dancing in the breeze.

Joan: You are quoting Wordsworth.

Pencil: Don't you like daffodils?

This script, so lacking in the ease and coherence of Stephen's philosophical discussions, would seem, at first glance, to be wholly valueless. But Joan and I have learned that the obstacles of subconsciousness frequently give to really evidential messages an appearance of worthlessness. We doubled the script up and forwarded it to Mrs. K. Her reply said, in part:

"When I began reading your script I said to myself, 'I don't know anybody named Charles.' Then came 'wading in a brook—no, brooks.' And there flashed into my mind that a very dear and intimate friend of Mr. K.'s was named Charles Brooks."

The chance of Joan ever having known of such a friendship was so remote that Mrs. K. did not suggest a subconscious explanation. Yet, after all, "Charles Brooks" was a mere inference on Mrs. K.'s part; the word " Charles" had been written, and the phrase "wading in brooks." The inference is interesting. But is one justified in definitely concluding that Charles Brooks was the communicator or even that the "pencil" intended to suggest his name?

"Necktie" meant nothing to Mrs. K., she said; she had never accused her husband of being "fussy." Did the quotation from Wordsworth mean anything?

Joan and I, looking the lines up, found them in the little poem "I Wandered Lonely as a Cloud," the first stanza of which reads:

I wandered lonely as a cloud
That floats on high o'er vales and hills,
When all at once I saw a crowd,
A host, of golden daffodils;
Beside the lake, beneath the trees,
Fluttering I "laughing" in the communication and dancing in the breeze.

We read the entire poem through time and time again, hoping to discover a purpose behind its being dragged into the script. We could find none. And the fact that the communicator had asked

Joan, "Don't you like daffodils?" seemed as pointless as the quotation itself.

Then on the evening of March 15th Stephen, communicating mentally, said: "Tell Mrs. K. that her husband has not forgotten the many yellow flowers she bloomed in the spring. Tell Mrs. K. to think on daffodils."

Stephen's words were mailed to Mrs. K. In a hurried reply, received by Joan March 18th, Mrs. K. said:

"I have raised daffodils in the house every spring for nearly twenty years, and they have been quite notable among my friends."

At last it looked as though Joan's and Mrs. K.'s correspondence had got somewhere. The Wordsworth quotation had acquired a very definite meaning. Unless it could be shown that knowledge of Mrs. K.'s daffodils was a part of the forgotten store of Joan's mind, the evidence that some extraneous agency was at work would be, to use Mrs. K.'s words, "most important."

Writing more in detail on March 19th, Mrs. K. said:

"The statement relative to the daffodils I raised in the spring is important; and yet I have to admit that there is a possible explanation. My daffodils were occasionally noticed in a local paper, which you might have seen. I hasten to say that it is my instinctive conviction that neither you nor Darby ever did see these notices. Yet the publicity given my narcissi catches me by the ankle just as I start to run with freedom!"

Again that vexing riddle—what is and isn't in Joan's subconscious mind! Again Joan can say that to the best of her belief she never read a word regarding Mrs. K.'s daffodils.

And, I think, something further can be said. The first daffodil suggestion was contained in the quotation from Wordsworth. This quotation itself did not mention daffodils, but was taken from a stanza that does. Stephen has said that the concrete is most difficult to communicate, because it tends to awaken the latent memories of the receiving station's own mind. But he has also indicated that, in order to catch the receiving station's subliminal off guard, it is sometimes necessary to employ roundabout methods, that the store of the subconscious, though so often an obstacle to communication, offers, nonetheless, one of the roundabout ways by which the concrete may sometimes be communicated.

Let us assume that Mr. K. was actually seeking to identify himself to Mrs. K. and for that purpose desired to use the word "daffodils." Had he come out with the word pointblank, Joan's subliminal might have traveled off on a personal tangent, relating such experiences of her own as the word suggested; and narration of these experiences might have entirely blocked the word. Instead of running this risk, Mr. K., let us say, found in Joan's mind memory of Wordsworth's daffodil poem; it was easy for Mr. K. to influence Joan and the pencil to write a quotation from this poem; the lines were quite impersonal. Once the verses were written the daffodils became a logical consequence. Mr. K. could then ask Joan with safety, "Don't you like daffodils?" and so, after much indirection, clinch the matter, preparing the way for Stephen to tell, without difficulty, of the many yellow flowers Mrs. K. had been wont to raise in the spring.

Shall we say that Joan must have known of Mrs. K.'s daffodils and forgotten them? Does the fact that they had been given a little publicity force us to that conclusion? Or shall we say that the unusual manner with which the daffodil suggestion was made, not directly as though coming from Joan, but most indirectly, indicates a something unsatisfactorily explained by the blanket assumption that Joan must have known?

Certainly we shall be tempted to say that something other than Joan's subliminal is indicated by "my hand," also contained in the automatic writing of March 11th. It failed at the time to impress Mrs. K. This is not to be greatly wondered at; for the communicator's exclamation, "My hand!", though thrice repeated, lacked definiteness and was unconnected with anything else in the script. With a previous message, the one we have named "any husband to any wife," it proved to have a most intimate connection.

XII

THE PLASTER HAND

"DURING those weeks of February and 'March, when Joan and Mrs. K. were keeping the post so busy, there was no thought on the part of either that they might meet. Yet they did. Unexpectedly Mrs. K. was called upon to make a trip to the West. On her way home she would be within a hundred miles of the city where Joan and I lived. Joan asked her to spend a week-end with us. And so we met her on the morning of March 29th. She was with us that day and part of the next.

Seating herself at Joan's desk the morning of March 29th, Mrs. K. fell to reading a record I had made of mental communication received on the 23d.

This communication had been invited with the thought that Stephen might be able to clear up some of the earlier Mrs. K. messages, for the ultimate veridicality of which Joan and I, in view of the daffodil development, had begun to hope. I quote a portion of the record:

Question By Darby: What about the "woman who sat in the barn" and "any husband to any wife"?

Stephen: Both of these messages were from David to his wife.

Darby: And yet she doesn't recognize them.

Stephen: In the second message ["any husband to any wife"] call "hand" to her attention. [Then came another than Stephen. Let us assume it was Mr. K.]

Mr. K.: Cast—cast—plaster—Over a grocery-store with outside steps built after the fire.

Stephen (interrupting): Now, Joan! Don't take that last down, Darby. Yes, take it down. It will show you again what the subconscious mind does.

Darby (recognizing that the grocery-store, etc., was possibly an outcropping of Joan's subliminal): Well, what about this dormer window business?

Mr. K. (apparently): A great window divided into three parts—fancy at the top— bookshelves—many books, many books. My hand.

And then Joan had begun a conversation of her own with the communicator. One can overhear but one side of a telephone conversation, so I could take notes only on what Joan said. "Well, I told your wife about the barn. She said there wasn't any barn." (Apparent difficulty of understanding on Joan's part.) "But what hills? . . . Oh, back from the river. Yes, and the river lies so. River comes down here." (Joan pointed her finger.) "Empties. Coast. Three towns. One back of river. . . . Mackport harbor here." (More pointing.) "Hills. Barn."

Then the communicator spoke. He said: " My yacht had red sails. Florence. Florence."

From time to time as she read the record, Mrs. K. exclaimed under her breath. What caused the exclamations? Several things. There were, for instance, the Mackeysport details. Granted Joan had seen the name of this town in the dedication of some book or other of Mrs. K.'s, where had her further knowledge come from? The Mackeysport community, Mrs. K. informed us, did consist of three settlements; there were hills and a river, and the latter did "empty." The description manifestly was confused, yet it offered definite facts. And note the "barn." Could this be the barn in which "the woman sat"?

"My yacht had red sails. Florence. Florence." These words Mrs. K. read aloud.

"Yes," she said, "his boat did have red sails."

So here were the yellow sails, possibly yellow, become red sails. Yellow sails had been without meaning to Mrs. K. But red sails? Why, of course! Yet what could Florence mean? Or what, if anything, did "Venice" of the original "yellow sail" message mean? "Venice, no," just as it had been "yellow, no." What was the meaning of Florence?

Later in the day Mrs. K. suddenly cried: "I have it. The name of Mr. K.'s boat was Tessa."

"But what has that to do with Florence?" I asked.

"Don't you remember!" Mrs. K. answered. "The scene of George Eliot's Romola is Florence. Tessa, you recall, is one of the novel's characters. Mr. K. was very fond of Romola and I remember that he named the boat after Tessa. The connection between the word 'Florence' in the communication and the actual name of Mr. K.'s boat is obvious."

This, I think, is very intriguing. The name "Tessa," it is evident, would be difficult to communicate, possibly for something of the same reason that it would be a hard word to convey to a partially deaf person or to a friend over the telephone; it is unusual. The word "Florence," on the other hand, is familiar to every one. Let us suppose Mr. K. actually was trying to communicate the name of his boat.

Unable to get "Tessa" through, he decided to communicate the word "Florence," thinking Mrs. K. would be able to put two and two together, just as, in fact, she seems to have done. His first effort failed. Instead of Joan speaking the word "Florence," she spoke the word "Venice." Why?

Suppose a yacht was under discussion between two friends and the name of an Italian city was mentioned by one of them in connection with the yacht. Suppose that the second person had been unable clearly to distinguish the name of the city. What Italian city might he infer was meant? Venice, of course—Venice with its canals and boats.

Whatever evidence is offered by the yacht with the red sails is strengthened, I feel, by the fact that the original message gave the yacht yellow sails. I regard the mistake of the first message, apparent at the time, as testimony that Joan was reaching out for a new fact rather than seeking to revive knowledge dormant in her subconsciousness. And yet, if the evidential quality of a communication is vitiated by its subject-matter having received publicity, then the evidence offered by the boat with the red sails vanishes, no matter how certain Joan may be that she never before heard of Mr. K.'s boat.

Mrs. K.'s sifting resulted finally in this statement: "Florence and the red sails seem to me important. Back in the '90's Mr. K. had a little boat with a lateen rig. The sail was dyed a russet red. But it is a fact that this little boat figured in occasional newspaper paragraphs, because the rig was unusual and the sail, on account of its color, striking."

The next comment made by Mrs. K., as she sat reading my notes on the communication of March 23d, was upon the words: "A great window divided into three parts—fancy at the top—bookshelves—many, many books."

This seems to hark back to the "dormer window," which was not a dormer window, but rather simply a big window. The big window, appearing in an early message, had been one of the things Mrs. K. had been loath to let go of. Had not Mr. K. been an admirer of spacious windows? And here the window was again, this time with detail. The detail was accurate. In a house in which the K's. lived for many years there was a long window, "divided into three parts, fancy at the top."

"The description," Mrs. K. said, "seems to me extraordinarily accurate." Then she added: "Architecturally the arrangement of the window was so unusual that a picture of it was reproduced in a magazine interested in interior decoration."

But Joan had no recollection of ever having seen that magazine. As for "the woman who sat in the barn"—had there been any barn pictures? That woman, in fact, was—Mrs. K. The incident was of so long ago that Mrs. K. had practically forgotten it. The first message that mentioned the barn failed to recall the facts of the case to her memory, seemingly because the description of the grounds did not tally with the yard in which the barn actually stood. For clearness I again quote the "woman who sat in the barn" message:

"There is a cottage in the midst of a garden. A sandy road. There are tall flowers. A pathway from the garden beds to the barn. A woman sat in the barn."

The attempt that was made to revise this message was not, it will be remembered, especially successful, though it did add this detail: "An upper window that overlooked the garden between the cliffs, at which you used to sit and write." We finally showed this new detail to Mrs. K., and it, together with the appearance of the word "barn" in the Mackeysport portion of the communication of March 23d, set her thinking. Here are the facts of the barn as she finally gave them to us:

"In 1891 or 1892 my husband rented a cottage at the seashore, and connected with it was a little barn. I used to write in the loft of this barn. Looking from one of the windows of this loft, across a little inlet of water, I could see some low banks or cliffs." (It will be recalled that the communicator had indicated dissatisfaction with the word "cliffs.") "There was, however, no garden connected with this place. But in the case of the Mackeysport house, which Mr. K. finally bought, and in which we lived, in the summer, for many years, there is a garden, but there is no barn. The message, as added to, seems to offer a composite description of the two localities."

Discarding the evidential possibilities of the composite description, we have left the fact that nearly twenty years ago Mrs. K. did sit in a barn and write—certainly an unusual thing to do. And here is an incident that seems to have received no printed mention! Here is an event in Mrs. K.'s life, communicated by one purporting to be Mr. K., which, there is every reason to believe, was not in Joan's subconsciousness, and which, in view of the fact that very rarely does a woman sit in a barn and write, can scarcely be explained on the basis of guess or coincidence. The communicated statement of this event was marred only by being linked with other less convincing statements.

Consider now the reiteration, from time to time, of the word "hand," culminating in: "Cast—cast—plaster." This, it seems, is the ideal test—a statement of fact that we know could not have

107

been in Joan's subliminal, a thing guess or coincidence cannot explain, a message untainted by surrounding inaccuracy. "Cast—cast—plaster" did stir Joan's own subconscious associations; but not until the words were safely through, making clear what hand, did subconsciousness inject its own associations. The whole offered a convincing piece of evidence, all the more convincing because, without the fact of the case being affected in the least, the color of Joan's subconscious memories was called forth. In other words, the test was not too good to be true.

"Cast—cast—plaster," ran my record. Instantly Mrs. K. saw the significance of "my hand"! She told us that many years ago, twenty, perhaps, or maybe twenty-five, her husband had had a plaster cast of his hand made for her.

"I very rarely see it now," she said. "I put it away, for fear it might be broken. . . . 'D-av-i' might have been the result of Joan's subconscious memory, of a name she had once seen and forgotten. So might 'Mack-port' and so might 'm-d-s-e.' Even the daffodils and the red sails and the big window may be such. But the plaster hand cannot be traced back to any normal explanation. Joan never could have known about it. Its appearance in the communication could not possibly have been the product of her subconscious memory."

And such, after time to think the matter over and permit interest to cool, remains Mrs. K.'s conviction. She has said, recently, "The plaster hand seems to me the one final, unquestionable test."

Of the four messages I asked you to carry in mind, three have proved evidential: "The woman who sat in the barn," "big window," and "yellow sail." What of the fourth message—"any husband to any wife?"

This sentence, you will recall, was embedded in the husband's letter: "The image of my hand, which you see, is not so real as the hand I lay on your hair, which you don't see."

To what hand and what image reference was here made is now apparent. But why was this original mention of the hand buried in "any husband to any wife" banalities? To one accepting Stephen's exposition of coloring, the answer would seem plain. The "image of my hand" was slipped through with a caution calculated to distract the mind of the receiving station from anticipation of a test. Note now what happened in the communication of March 23d, when Mrs. K.'s husband risked being more definite:

"Cast—cast—plaster. Over a grocery-store with outside steps built after the fire." Whereupon Stephen interrupted, saying: "Now, Joan! Don't take that last down, Darby.

Yes, take it down. It will show you again what the subconscious mind does."

When Joan was in college, one of the buildings was damaged by fire, and the class in art was housed temporarily in a room over a grocery-store. The room was reached by outside steps, built after the fire. To this improvised class-room were moved the plaster casts of the art department. And this set of facts, stored away in Joan's subconsciousness, was stirred to life by Mr. K.'s "cast—cast—plaster." Here, then, is constituted a most interesting example of coloring, interesting because so apparent and because it in no way affects the accuracy of the connotation which "cast—cast—plaster" gave to "hand."

Is there anything to be gained by discussion of the part telepathy may have played in the "plaster hand" message or the "woman who sat in the barn" message or any of the others, if in view of all the facts related they seem not to have sprung from Joan's subliminal?

One can assert that the facts of all of these messages were in Mrs. K.'s mind, and that possibly they were transferred from her mind to Joan's. But after that assertion has been made, what further can be said? Anything may be possible—even the chance that Stephen is what he says he is, and that his philosophy came to Joan and me from real, though discarnate intelligence. And when we consider the world's limited experience with the phenomenon of telepathy, I am not so sure that the telepathic explanation is less forced than the thought that Mrs. K.'s search for her lost husband had to a degree proved successful.

XIII

THE LITTLE GRAY DRESS

AFTER Mrs. K. had finished reading the communications of March 23d, I showed her a few of the many messages we had received from the professor. She told us she had known him somewhat, and I was eager to learn whether the character and atmosphere of the real professor and the purported one agreed. Our professor was of a speech that would have been a little pompous except for its quizzical humor. Always he addressed me as "my dear sir," and always, it seemed, he was as much amused by his formality as was I. Joan and I had not known the professor when he lived here.

"It suggests him," Mrs. K. announced, after I had read an example or two of the professor's way of putting things; but she added that her acquaintance with the professor had not been intimate.

"Here is something," I said, "that came as long ago as February, 1917. I am sure the professor, when he was living, never carried on in such fashion."

For several days prior to receipt of this particular communication, Stephen had been saying he thought the time was coming when, under the conditions of direct mental communication, Joan would be able to see him. He said she would remember nothing about the experience afterward, but at the time she would be able to tell something of what she saw, not much, perhaps, because words would be lacking.

On the February evening in question, Joan interrupted the communication to say, "Well, I can see now."

I sat silent, awaiting developments, and finally she went on, at one moment addressing the communicator, and at others half-soliloquizing:

"There is a man sitting on the arm of my chair, and I can see right through him. I don't know him, but he is nice. He has twinkly eyes. Oh, is it the professor? Well, I don't think you ought to sit on the arm of my chair. You say there are no conventions? Why not? Well, you don't need to laugh so hard. His laugh is beautiful. The professor says it is permissible for him to sit on the side of my chair. There are several persons standing around the professor. Stephen is not here. He is busy. They all look about the same age, except when they make pictures for me." (What Joan seems to have meant by "they make pictures for me" is interesting; I shall quote Stephen on this matter later.)

Then the professor himself broke in, saying to me: "I am hugging your wife. Perfectly permissible, my dear sir!"

Now if Joan and I had tried to imagine the professor as he was in this life, a by-play such as I have related would never have entered our minds. The professor was a man of dignified learning. Yet, said Mrs. K., "I can imagine him saying just that sort of droll thing."

And then Joan adjusted a handkerchief to her eyes. She wears a blindfold during mental communication to protect her sight from the light of the room. I touched Joan's wrist.

The first word that came was "Fern." It was spelled out, then pronounced several times. The next words were: "A girl at Fern." There was nothing more concerning "Fern" until near the close of the second period of the afternoon's communication.

I should state here that during Mrs. K.'s visit with us there were four separate periods of communication, two on the afternoon of March 29th, one on the evening of the same day, and one on the following morning.

Near the close of the afternoon's second period these words came: "Fern Hill."

A copy of my notes on the messages of March 29th and 30th was forwarded Mrs. K. after she reached home, with the request that she comment definitely on whatever evidential matter the communications contained. Acting on her usual impulse to avoid a supernormal explanation when a normal one will answer, Mrs. K. writes of "Fern Hill" thus:

"As a girl I attended a boarding-school called Fern Hill. It has been out of existence for years. But I have been the subject of occasional biographical sketches, and in some of them Fern Hill is mentioned."

Again and again possible subconscious knowledge on Joan's part! And yet the given individual reads but little of the many biographical facts printed concerning this person or that. Joan has no recollection of ever having read anything biographical of Mrs. K.; no memory of her conscious mind is stirred by the words "Fern Hill."

Nor has Joan recollection of ever having known the facts contained in the following message, delivered to Mrs. K., not by Stephen or the professor, but by one other who comes to Joan and me frequently: "You were a bit of a lass when you went to another house; not your father's. Your mother came here where I am, and your father, too. You went away —a bit lass. They were your own people, but not your father or mother."

Mrs. K. writes: "On the death of my mother, at my birth, I was taken into the family of an aunt, with whom I lived until I was seventeen or eighteen years old. My father died when I was a child."

The possibility that Joan possessed subconscious knowledge of these facts is surely most remote. And the same comment may be made on the following:

Some one came who spoke the name "Dick." A personality thus named often comes to Joan and me, and so I answered by saying, "Hello, Dick!" But the communicator replied, "Not your Dick," and then continued with the appearance of addressing Mrs. K., saying: "Royce. Hodgson." (Both names were spelled out, Hodgson being spelled incorrectly—"Hodgeson.") "I only wanted to tell you that after all our discussions Royce and I have come to the same conclusions at last. We don't fight any more; not that we weren't always good friends." There was a pause. Then he who seemed to desire to be known as Hodgson uttered two words: "Brown coat."

Mrs. K., much amused, said that she did, indeed, remember Dr. Hodgson's brown coat.

She added: "I do not know of any particular relationship between the late Professor Royce of Harvard and Doctor Hodgson, although, of course, it is reasonable to suppose that they knew each other, and they may easily have differed as to their deductions on psychic phenomena. But that brown coat! Doctor Hodgson disapproved greatly of the somberness of men's evening dress. In order to protest against the convention he had a dress-suit made out of a brown broadcloth. It caused him to be rather conspicuous and greatly amused people. But he was dogged about it, and for a long time insisted on wearing the brown coat out to dinner."

Here was a fact known to people of one city, but too trivial to be generally known. If anything has been written about Doctor Hodgson's brown coat, it is practically certain that Joan never heard of it. Indeed, we knew only from Mrs. K. who Richard Hodgson was; one of her letters had mentioned him as a pioneer psychical investigator.

It should be said that not all the messages received on March 29th and 30th had meaning. For instance, the word "suit-case" was insisted on. It was as though an object was being shown Joan. Attempting to identify it, she said: "A suit-case. Most peculiar suit-case. Inside the suit-case? I can't see. I am sorry." Now, the suit-case meant nothing to Mrs. K., nor does it mean anything to Joan and me.

But, on the other hand, consider the episode of the picture. Joan, speaking in what seemed to be her own character, said: "You go into a hall. Then there's a curved stairway. Then a—which? ... A picture. Well, that is what I call a curved staircase. Spiral? All right. Is it your picture?"

The K. home, Mrs. K. says, has a curving stairway. I do not feel, though, that any considerable degree of evidence is thereby offered, because, in the first place, the stairway details of the communication are rather indefinite; in the second place, any house might have a curving staircase. This last could be said of the "picture," too (after all, it is not surprising that there was a portrait of Mr. K. in his own home), except for the fact that a subsequent message described the man pictured.

The foregoing mention of the "picture" occurred in the first period of communication. In the course of the second period, Joan said, apparently addressing Mr. K.: "You don't look like a business man; you look like a professional man. You know, you look not unlike my father. Yes, father wore a Vandyke, too. In the picture? I see. On the landing."

Now, as a matter of fact, a picture of Mr. K. did hang on the landing of Mrs. K.'s home. And though during the years immediately before his death Mr. K. did not wear a beard, at the time the portrait on the landing was made he did — a Vandyke. Further, after I had signaled Joan that the period of communication was over, and read my notes to her, she brought her father's picture. Mrs. K. was impressed by the resemblance between her husband and Joan's father. She writes:

"The photograph which Joan showed me strongly suggests Mr. K. as he looked before he shaved off his beard. There is the same broad brow. Except that the face is a little shorter than my husband's, and perhaps rounder, the likeness is obvious."

The statement that Mr. K. looked like a professional man is also interesting. This remark, Mrs. K. told us, had been made during Mr. K.'s lifetime by many persons.

Another engaging bit of evidence was the "Washington" incident. It struck me as most interesting, because it exemplified so clearly how the subconscious mind of the receiving station can cloud a fact, and yet later so clear it that its evidential character is with difficulty gainsaid.

During the evening of March 29th the name "Washington" was spelled out incorrectly, in this fashion: "W-a-s-h-i-n-g-e-t-o-n." Then came the numbers "four, five"; and then they came again, only in the order "five, four." That was all at the time. Toward the close of the evening's communication Joan spoke as follows: "Four, five; five, four. I can't tell which goes first. Washington."

To me, and, when I read Joan my notes, to her also, "Washington" and the combination of numbers were an enigma. On the morning of March 30th Mrs. K. and I were alone together for a while. We discussed the communications of the day before, and finally she said: "There is something I would like to tell you."

"Better not," I answered. "If anything has come that isn't altogether clear, give it a chance to straighten itself out in to-day's communication."

And so Mrs. K. said nothing.

And the very first word Joan spoke after I touched her wrist that morning was "Potomac." She followed it with "four, five," and then started to change the numbers to "five, four." But Mrs. K. said: "Five-four is right."

After communication had been brought to a close, Mrs. K. told us that twenty years ago she and Mr. K. lived at 54 Potomac Street. The possibility of Joan ever having read or been told that Mrs. K. had lived, years ago, at such and such a number on such and such a street, is so remote that it scarcely exists.

One more test was offered to Mrs. K.—in the course of the second period of the communication of the afternoon of March 29th. It was preceded by the following, purporting to be addressed by Mr. K. to his wife:

"There is much work for you. There is quantity you must bring as your gift. When you understand you will be content. You can work for me—still in partnership. You cannot want to do other than fulfil your possibilities of service. You see there is not only yourself to think of; there is your relation to the whole. The relationship between the individual and the body social is very close."

A bit more came in this vein. Then suddenly Mr. K. broke off to say: "I wish you would wear your gray dress. Couldn't you?"

Mrs. K. smiled. "It is worn out," she said.

"You could get another one," Mr. K. urged.

Concerning this brief conversation, Mrs. K. writes: "The reference to the gray dress is, I think, in the plaster-cast class of evidence, or possibly even one better. Before I was married I had a little cheap gray flannel dress which Mr. K. liked very much. He liked it so much that he wanted me to wear it when I was married! You can imagine how a girl, with visions of white satin, replied to the suggestion."

Surely the "gray dress" possesses a certain evidential value, despite the fact that other women have had gray dresses which have been admired by their husbands. But Mrs. K. continues:

"On May 11, 1918, the eve of the anniversary of my marriage, I and another operated a ouija-board. The pointer made some reference to my wedding anniversary, and then said: 'Wanted you to wear gray dress.' This had absolutely no meaning for me. I had entirely forgotten that there ever had been a gray dress, and so I said: 'I don't remember anything about a gray dress.' Then said the board: 'That is what I want. If you remember, you do not believe.'

"That Joan, nearly a year later, should have spoken the words 'I wish you would wear your gray dress,' is most impressive. By no possible stretch of the imagination can that be credited to her subliminal!"

XIV

THE LIMIT OF EVIDENCE

EVIDENTIAL tests can eliminate, perhaps, that explanation of psychic communication that is based on theories of the subconscious mind. Tests can eliminate the telepathic theory. They can narrow things down to a point where seemingly only the spiritistic explanation is left. And then— even then it is possible to reject survival of the dead.

Rejection in such a case results from a rigorous interpretation of the rules of testimony. Even legal inquiry does not ignore prima facie evidence; it requires that such presumptive evidence be rebutted. But legal inquiry seeks to prove only that which is of ordinary experience. Psychic proof of the survival of the dead involves extraordinary experiences. Therefore, whoever wishes to insist on a strict interpretation of the rules of evidence has right to this statement:

One can admit that a Joan voices facts extraneous to her own knowledge, or to a Darby's or an F. W.'s or a Mrs. K.'s, and yet reasonably demand further proof, positive rather than negative, of the dead that live.

For instance, the evidence offered by the plaster hand does not conclusively prove that Mrs. K.'s lost husband is found. It can be relied upon to prove only that in some unexplained manner Joan can tell of facts beyond her own knowledge. And I am not convinced that the plaster hand by itself can be depended on even to that extent. It eliminates the subconscious explanation only when it is supported by the entire mass of the Mrs. K. communication.

Again, the F. W. messages do not prove conclusively that Uncle Michael survives. They simply eliminate telepathy. Joan, it would appear, has ability not only to voice facts outside her own knowledge, but outside that also of persons en rapport with her.

But it may be said that, granted the Mrs. K. and F. W. messages constitute no actual proof of survival, they do nonetheless evidence it. Certainly this is so. The Mrs. K. and F. W. messages evidence survival to the degree that their elimination of contrary explanations is complete. But here there is a fresh difficulty, namely:

The psychic evidence of survival that touches you personally impresses you. Evidence that doesn't touch you personally is, so far as you are concerned, less impressive. Let F. W. attach what weight he will to the Uncle Michael messages; you to whom these messages are wholly impersonal will grant them less importance.

To Joan and me the F. W. and Mrs. K. messages seem less convincing than Fred Q.'s successful claim to identity with Frederick Gaylord of The *Seven Purposes* and Stephen's identification of himself as Stephen L——. Somehow these two occurrences were personal to us in a way that neither the F. W. nor Mrs. K. messages were; they seem our particular property. To us, indeed, the Mrs. K. and F. W. messages are cold facts, personally important because they give support to

Fred Q. as Frederick Gaylord and Stephen as Stephen L .

And Frederick Gaylord and Stephen L are important to Joan and me because they in their turn give support and authenticity to the coming of Stephen's philosophy.

In fact, of all the evidence external to the import of the philosophy itself, that has been offered Joan and me, the philosophy's mere coming, the ouija-board's performance as such, seems to us the most startling and most convincing.

If you sat down some evening to amuse yourself with a toy, a ouija-board, and the thing, actuated apparently by an agency outside yourself, began to spell out in orderly array a philosophy of life and death, would not such a performance, wholly aside from your ultimate acceptance or rejection of the philosophy, appeal to you as more evidential than John Smith's umbrella or, indeed, Stephen's identification? The ouija-board's bare performance lifts a coral reef such as Mrs. K.'s nearer to the surface of the waters—much nearer, Joan and I think!

Yet no sooner do Joan and I make ready to accept the tripod's performance as clinching, final evidence of life after death, no sooner do we start to run with freedom, to quote Mrs. K., than we are caught by the ankle. Strict interpretation of evidence trips us up. However sure we may feel that it was not our subconscious minds that shot the tripod from letter to letter, or the mind of some one in telepathic rapport with us, we cannot conclude simply from that conviction that Stephen L is a living dead man. Elimination of subliminal and telepathic explanations of the tripod's performance supports the spiritistic explanation, but does not prove it.

Perhaps no conclusive evidence can be found. Perhaps all that evidence can do is to pile itself up, acquiring a cumulative force which, though it never positively proves survival, pushes so-called natural explanations of psychic communications farther and farther into the background. Or perhaps the content of Stephen's philosophy will achieve that which the mere phenomenon of its coming failed of. If the philosophy is reasonable, as the professor has said, in the light of men's already acquired knowledge, perhaps evidence external to it need be corroborative only.

In any event, Stephen's philosophy came to Joan and me unvouched for, with not a word for weeks about John Smith's umbrella. We could listen to the unauthenticated message, or pass it up. We chose to listen.

And so let us go back to that night in December, 1916, when I came home and found Joan's newly purchased toy hidden behind the trunk in the closet.

That night, for the second time in our lives, Joan and I placed our fingers on a ouija-board's pointer. Whether she was the psychic or I, if, indeed, the operation of a ouija-board required a psychic, we did not know. Direct mental communication was as yet undreamed of. Stephen's use of the word "coloring" was not in our vocabulary. Some weeks were to elapse before F. W. would catch our ouija-board red-handed. Mrs. K. was a mere name and was to remain so for over two years. The Seven Purposes was unwritten, and the communications it contains were not to be received for yet a year or more.

Joan and I sit with our hands on the ouija-board's tripod. It moves, as the tripod at Mrs. Jevon's boarding-house had moved a few nights before. Together Joan and I piece the words it spells into a sentence, and I record that sentence. Then again we place our fingers on the tripod, and again it moves. As it picks its way across the alphabet, we sit and watch it. We are fascinated, bewildered, half afraid.

I do not quite know how to correlate my facts. The truth of the matter is that each philosophy and religion had, and has, at least one fundamental fact. Many facts make the truth if you could only sift them from the emotional hypotheses. Of these many facts, man is at all times conscious of one, which is the central fact of all: Consciousness is, or, as one says, 'I am.' But man has allowed his emotions to color this central fact, to dress it out in hues that shift and change and like a will-o'-the-wisp lead him from the path of

I submit that if a ouija-board came at you in such a fashion you would be intrigued. "Emotional hypotheses," for instance! What could the phrase mean, if anything? Was it mere jargon?

"'Emotional hypotheses' will bear definition," I said, more than half suspecting that any attempt the ouija-board might make to define the high-sounding term would prove incoherent.

But promptly the tripod replied:

"By emotional hypothesis is meant that impatience which leads the egotistical minds of men to jump at a conclusion rather than undergo the strain and suspense of logical reasoning. The truth is so simple. But for man's emotional hypotheses he could have read it in the fields thousands of years ago. And because of earth's present scientific understanding of natural law it has become simpler than simple if men will but think clearly from the premises they have already established."

How absurd for me to sit there and address this less than shadowy Stephen! Yet I argued: "But science has fenced off the natural world from that other world religion calls spiritual."

"The material and the spiritual are closer than scholars have said," replied Stephen. "But grasp first the truth of all truths, consciousness. Consciousness is. Now the earth terms on which I am depending to make myself clear to you are, quantity and quality. Quantity and quality are the fundamentals of consciousness. First, though, is there any question you care to ask?"

Thus to lay down a principle or two and then call for comment was in the beginning a favorite method of Stephen's instruction.

"There are many questions," I said. "But I count myself a fool to interrogate a ouija-board."

"Oh, drat the ouija-board!" exclaimed Stephen. "You never mind the toy. Remember that the greatest physical force known, electricity, was discovered by means of a boy's kite."

"Well, then, Stephen," I said, "do all persons survive at death?"

"They become as I," he answered. "Still possessed of a degree of my own I am a part of the great consciousness. I am only a part of a whole, yet the whole is I. You do not understand; later this will be made clear to you. But don't use the word 'death.' Man has read into this word so much that is somber, so much of unhappiness and despair. The earth term that corresponds to our thought here of what you call death, is graduation.

And as I did not die, but rather graduated into a new mode of consciousness, so be assured that graduation, not death, awaits you."

Graduation? Here was another novel term. Surely neither Joan nor I were inventors of "quality," "quantity," "emotional hypothesis," "graduation."

Indeed, if by graduation Stephen meant a process of dying whereby one leaps at a bound into eternal bliss, or, in case one has sinned greatly, into eternal damnation, I must oppose him.

"To me," I said, "that notion has always seemed fishy."

"Whaley!" came back the ouija-board, with the ready pithiness which quickly made Stephen's personality appear so normal.

"I have graduated into a higher consciousness," the tripod continued. "By this I do not mean that I have reached the height of consciousness. My present degree is much the same as yours and that of Joan. But between that part of a given degree of consciousness which is on your side and that part of the same degree which is on my side, there is this difference: Here we do not see as through a glass darkly. We recognize ourselves here as a whole, and perfection is the end."

"Then, Stephen," I asked, "you will in the future become different from what you are now? Will you die again?"

"Yes," he responded, "though by 'die' you mean 'graduate.'"

"But men have such an unholy fear of death," I said.

"Unholy? Yes and no," Stephen replied. "Unholy because they do not understand the truth. Holy because earth-life is their opportunity to develop the quantity of consciousness."

As I wrote down Stephen's words, I said to Joan: "Now you have two riddles—quality of consciousness and also quantity. And quantity I think is the more puzzling of the two." How might the word quantity be applied to consciousness? When we touched the tripod again it spelled:

"Understanding of consciousness, and of its quality and quantity, is essential to the progress of this revelation. So also must you understand the degrees of consciousness."

Stephen's second dying had gripped Joan's interest.

"Tell me!" she urged. "You say your future holds new experiences, new graduations. Does not this create uncertainty and doubt, even for you?"

"Why should I fear?" Stephen answered. "My second graduation, my third, my fourth, my fifth, each I shall recognize as a promotion, just as my first graduation was a promotion. On the one hand, I shall graduate many, many times into ever higher degrees of consciousness, reaching ultimately the supreme degree. On the other hand, a part of the whole is constantly reborn."

At mention of rebirth Joan, the practical, tilted her nose to an elevation a shade above normal. "I thought it was about time for that hocus-pocus of reincarnation to make its appearance!" she muttered.

"Stephen," I put in, "you have said that each philosophy and religion shadows forth a fundamental fact. Is rebirth the fundamental truth of the Oriental doctrine of transmigration of the soul?"

"But surely," the ouija-board replied.

"Do you mean to tell us," Joan asked, "that you existed prior to your earth existence?"

"But surely," the ouija-board repeated.

"Stephen," I said, joining in Joan's impatience, "as I recall the transmigration idea it holds that souls leaving the bodies of men are sometimes reborn into the bodies of animals, and vice versa. Surely you do not mean that we should take such a mad notion seriously?"

"I have not said so," Stephen answered. "Stop and recall my definition of emotional hypothesis. The transmigration thought is but a guess at the truth, a theory in some measure correct, yet highly colored by emotional reasoning."

"But you still insist, do you, Stephen, that you will be born again into this world of men?" I questioned.

"Yes," he replied. "I am sure to be born again—it cannot be otherwise—yet not all of me as I knew myself before. But you do not understand. For the present accept the thought that consciousness is constantly reborn. Then accept this fact: The individual, once graduated from earthly existence, never again returns as an individual. As an individual he goes on and on; ever nearer he approaches and ultimately reaches supremacy. These two thoughts may now seem contradictory. The contradiction will disappear when you understand what I mean by rebirth."

"Well," I said, "may I ask this—are you glad you died?"

"Had I remained longer on the earth plane," Stephen spelled in reply, "I would have had greater opportunity to develop the quantity of my consciousness. Yet here I can develop quality of consciousness, with which to be born again into your world in order there to develop quantity."

In my first effort to record this speech I became confused, and so asked Stephen to repeat his words.

"Anything to oblige," he replied. And again the speech, entire, spelled itself out.

I have said that the mere performance of the tripod has appealed to Joan and me as evidence that the philosophy had origin in mind other than our own. Now and then some long sentence would complete itself only to find us forgetful of its first half. Entire clauses would be missing. We would cudgel our brains to remember them, and when we failed the tripod, without hesitation, would repeat the sentence. Such occurrences added but a mite to the bigger marvel—the logic with which the performing tripod, starting with a few definitions, developed its thought into a rounded-out system, finishing one subject, then passing on to the next, until finally the work was done.

But Stephen's twice-spelled speech had awakened rebellion in my practical Joan. "Where's all this stuff leading to?" she demanded to know. "What's the point of it? And it contradicts itself! If the dead are reborn, why don't they bring back to earth the knowledge they acquire while they're dead?"

As she spoke we replaced our fingers on the tripod. It moved quickly across the board.

"I, rather the quality of my consciousness," it spelled, "will bring back a greater power to assimilate mortal experience; that is, to develop quantity."

"Your answer is evasive," charged Joan. "Put it this way—when you were here, why did you not remember your previous earth experiences? You didn't, I suppose. I am sure I don't remember ever having had a previous existence."

"I did have glimpses," Stephen responded, "just as you have glimpses of previous earth existence. The first time I went to England there were certain places that were startlingly familiar. All people who travel have this experience more or less. Then often I experienced that feeling, common to every one, of having previously done things which were, as a matter of fact, quite new. Then, too, some things were easier for me to learn and understand than others. And here is another term we shall have frequent occasion to use— glimpse. Men have had many glimpses."

"It is interesting!" exclaimed Joan.

"The fairy-tale of Aladdin and his wonderful lamp is a glimpse," the tripod continued. "Aladdin had only to rub the lamp and the genie would appear. You have but to call and I am with you. Glimpses are not really essential to my revelation, yet they will prove suggestive once you have learned to recognize them. Store the glimpse-thought away with those other ideas— consciousness, quality of consciousness, quantity of consciousness, degrees of consciousness, and rebirth of consciousness."

I objected, declaring myself unequal to it all.

"So you say," replied Stephen. "Yet to you is being given this revelation—not so entirely by me as you think. There are many others, of higher degree, interested. In fact, this is the greatest of happenings to us here. . . . Poor you!"

The words "poor you" seemed drawled out, the tripod creeping tantalizingly at a snail's pace.

"Yet for all your mock sympathy," said I, "adequate understanding of the riddles you are propounding would require hours and days of thought."

"Consider the necessary thinking in the light of a recreation," Stephen answered. "Consider how nimble such exercise will make your mind. But pardon me, old top, if I ask you to store one more thought away—the idea of supremacy, the supreme degree of consciousness."

"What we call God?" I asked.

"God is consciousness," Stephen replied. "Consciousness is God. Consciousness is within you. God is within you. The germ of supremacy is yours and is mine and is in all things animate and inanimate. Consciousness is. It is all there ever was or will be, without beginning and without end."

"Stephen," I offered, "you indicate that, perhaps, supremacy has been reached by certain individuals. Who are some of these?"

"Christ," the answer came, "and most of those whom the world calls saints."

"Was Christ, then, just a man?" I asked.

"What else should he have been?" Stephen replied. "Yet he was in your world as the result of the rebirth of a degree of quality approaching the supreme. And he so fulfilled his quantity that his earth graduation was his last. He passed directly into supremacy."

The tripod paused, then began swaying back and forth. From one side of the board to the other it moved, then up and down, and finally it spelled, "Good night." For two or three minutes we sat waiting further word, but the genie was gone. Joan carried the board and tripod to the closet, then said:

"I'm not sure that I really know what's meant by one's subconscious mind. But I'll chance the opinion that we've just been observing such a mind at work."

"Whose?" I asked.

"Why, yours," she answered. Then added, "But where did your subconscious mind get such ideas!"

XVI

THE NEW LAW OF PARALLELS

THE subconscious mind was not, of course, the author of Stephen's philosophic discourse; this subsequently was made clear by our discovery that Joan, not I, was the psychic. At the time, though, it did seem that, if the phenomenon of Stephen's philosophy was to be explained on a basis of subconsciousness, my subliminal, not Joan's, was implicated Joan had never read a line of metaphysics; I had. Certainly I had neither read nor independently contrived the thoughts the ouija-board gave expression to. Nonetheless, I detected in Stephen's words an evolutionary viewpoint that, in a way, seemed to crystallize certain vague ideas of my own.

Joan and I have been of the Sunday-morning go-to-church type. Her attendance was sincere; the church answered satisfactorily enough such questions concerning life as she cared to ask. I attended because Joan did and because, in truth, the church answered many of my own questions. But occasionally the sermons offended me greatly, especially when they carried reference to man as a "fallen creature."

It seemed to me inconceivable that religion could so lag behind laboratory truths. When would the church forget its ancient tradition? Could it not perceive that man is a risen creature, that throughout the ages he has struggled always upward, that, instead of having origin in a state of perfection from which in the perverseness of his heart he fell, he was formed in a state of undevelopment out of which he is evolving perfection? Man, I knew, has climbed well, considering that when he started the ascent he was not man at all, but an immeasurably low form of life. He would, I believed, continue to climb.

But this belief of mine was not wholly cheering. After all, evolution promised a glorious future only to mankind. Death, so far as I could see, cut short the individual man's progress summarily enough.

Indeed, there was really no great resemblance between my thought and Stephen's. He, like the church, was victor over death; I had ceased to hope for individual immortality. How could my subconsciousness differ so radically from my conscious conclusions?

Subconscious mind or no, with Stephen relating God up to what he termed the supreme degree of consciousness, with his postulating the germ of supreme consciousness in all animate things, and inanimate, it seemed quite the most natural thing in the world that I should ask, when next we talked with him, "Stephen, is the theory of evolution a glimpse?"

"There are two great glimpses," the ouija-board answered. "Evolution is one of these. In his social development man had courted differentiation. Out of the simplicity of tribal life he has evolved the complexities of civilization. The race has unconsciously followed the law which your modern scientist has consciously checked up: Out of the simple, the complex; out of the lower degree, the higher."

133

"True," I said, "but what help is that to the individual Joan and the individual me? Through evolution the race may become perfect. But Joan and I, we die."

"Wait!" the tripod replied. "Your science knows but half of evolution. I hope to be able to explain to you, before long, the other half.

"Successful in the explanation of biological development, the theory of evolution gains wider and wider application in interpreting the special activities of life—politics, industry, the arts, religion. And in the so-called material sciences, in physics and chemistry, it is being more and more recognized as equally operative. In inorganic matter evolution finds one expression; in the reproductive processes of life, another; in the intellectual and moral phases of human endeavor, still another. Always it is the same law; its varying manifestations parallel each other. Now, here where I am there are laws, just as natural as yours—though you may prefer to term them supernatural—which parallel the laws, evolution included, of the earth-plane."

"Do you mean," I asked, "that spiritual law is simply a more complex expression of material law, and that the law of your plane is but a parallel of the natural or earth-plane law?"

"Parallelism, so defined," Stephen replied, "is the second of the two great glimpses, the greatest really of all glimpses. If earth scientists will free their minds of emotional hypotheses and interpret psychological laws on the basis of so-called material laws, they will lift assurance of the existence of my plane out of the field of mystic belief into that of reasonable fact."

I tossed the ouija-board aside.

"Food for thought, Joan!" I said. "You wouldn't care if I took a walk and tried to digest this Stephen thing's words?"

I put on my overcoat and stepped out into the snow. "' Now, here where I am,'" I quoted as I tramped along, ""there are laws, just as natural as yours, which parallel the laws, evolution included, of the earth-plane.'"

But the night was bright and the air bracing. The streets were alive with amusement-going traffic. And soon, under the commonplace influence of it all, I thought how musty it was to sit indoors philosophizing with a ouija-board. I hurried home and proposed a theater to Joan.

But when we returned we sat up until three in the morning, discussing Stephen's philosophy, whether it would hold out to a definite goal, and who, if not my subconscious mind, was its author. Stephen certainly was not Stephen!

XVII

"There Is No Death"

"A SUPPLY-TRAIN was blown up to-day by the Allies, and many boys were graduated. Battle, murder, and sudden death! The shock of sudden death in all its forms is so great. That is why peoples of older civilizations, glimpsing the truth, prayed to be spared it. This war is such a foolish waste of consciousness."

Thus spelled Stephen the evening following his remarks on evolution and the law of parallels.

In the course of Mrs. K.'s visit I ran through my record of the early communications, and by chance the foregoing speech was among the ouija-board spellings I read her.

"Did you verify the statement about the blowing up of the supply-train?" she asked, interested in the evidential possibility. She was disappointed when I answered, "No."

It occurred to neither Joan nor me in December, 1916, to attach importance to the "supply-train"—not as evidence. Stephen of the ouija-board had not yet proved that Stephen L was other than a mere name; and Joan and I had the vaguest notions of psychical research. If we were not sufficiently interested in evidential tests to seek verification of Stephen's death story, surely we would not think of verifying the "supply-train." It was the face value of Stephen's words that engaged our interest—the thought that the old stereotyped phrase of the prayer-book might have a hidden meaning.

"Are all persons frightened when they die?" Joan asked.

But for quite awhile no answer came. Finally the tripod spelled:

"This is Stephen. I was called away. I have told you my choice of work here—the meeting of frightened boys coming from the battle-fields. To-day I have been very busy. Do you remember the legend of the Valkyries, how they visited the battle-fields, revived the slain heroes, and bore them away to Valhalla? We on this side do not bodily carry the newcomers from Europe's modern trenches. Yet some ancient Norse minstrel had a glimpse of the truth when he sang the story of the Valkyries."

Joan then repeated her question, whether all persons are frightened when they die.

"Those only," answered Stephen, "who know sudden death. Otherwise, the larger consciousness reveals itself before graduation actually occurs, in what you call unconsciousness and death-bed visions. Sudden death is frightful only because a person does not know where he has gone. Sleep precedes natural death always, sometimes just for the space of a heart-beat. That second is long enough for the truth of graduation to be revealed."

"But," asked Joan, "does one reach full understanding immediately?"

"I have not said so," Stephen replied. "The new-born soul here is delicate, just as newly born earth life is delicate. How quickly the new-comer acquires full knowledge of the life here depends on his degree. With some we have what you might term trouble. The comprehension of such is not quick, as it was not quick in their earth life, and they torment themselves by insisting on going back to their familiar places. They are, of course, distressed because those whom they have left in the flesh fail to see them.

"As for the boys from the trenches, we often have trouble with them. They come with all the shock and horror of sudden death. Their first impulse is to go on fighting; more battles have been won by the strength of invisible forces than by flesh-and-blood troops — truly have the angels led on to victory. At other times a soldier-boy, finding himself free, makes straight for home."

"How does he travel?" I interrupted.

"I cannot explain to you in exact terms," the tripod spelled. "But have you ever boarded a train that was going to carry you to a dear friend whom you had not seen for a long time? Surely your thoughts outran that train. If your friend had been able, through some strange faculty, to have sensed those thoughts of yours, and you had been able to sense his, you would have arrived at your destination long before the train. Well, something of that sort is the case on my plane. As our thoughts shift, so, if we choose, do we ourselves shift, going where we will. You call and I come."

Stephen's "supply-train" speech had said, "This war is such a foolish waste of consciousness." I wanted to ask how this could be so if the dead survive. But the tripod seemed intent on finishing its discussion of sudden death. It continued:

"The soldier-boy, having reached home, is greatly grieved that his presence goes unnoted by those he loves. You see, he does not yet realize he has graduated. If we can get early control of those who come to us from the battlefield, and can take them to some quiet spot away from the upheaval, we are able to teach them quickly the truth and joy of their immortality."

"After all, then, even sudden death is not a tragedy of long duration?" said Joan.

"No," said Stephen, "nothing that is negative is of really long duration. Yet truly it is well for the world thoroughly to understand sudden death as a tragic horror.

"Let us say the head of a soldier-boy is shot off—an unpleasant thought, though an occurrence many times daily on the battle-fields of Europe. In a trice the boy is free from his body, and so sudden has been his passing that none is there to meet him. He will see what he recognizes as himself, lying mangled; yet he will feel himself alive. Perhaps he will recognize the dead body of a comrade, also just graduated. They see each other double, as it were. They begin communicating, both utterly bewildered. That is the horror—neither knows what has happened or where he is.

"It was truly a great glimpse that found its way into the prayer-book, 'From battle and murder, and from sudden death, good Lord, deliver us.' The peculiar thing is that, in the distant day of this prayer's origin, battle was man's highest glory and death in battle a soldier's fitting crown; yet the seers so far glimpsed the truth that they gave to man a prayer contradictory to his practice."

Stephen's gruesome recital had caused Joan to wince.

"Why so realistic, Stephen?" I asked.

"My friends," he spelled, "the world should know for two reasons. First, earth must adopt all safeguards for the prevention of sudden death. Its horror fully realized, men will minimize its occurrence, not only as the result of war, but also as the consequence of industrial greed or plain carelessness. Second, if men are warned and are made to understand, death coming suddenly will be robbed of much of its shock; there are times when true men would die in no other way than suddenly, if—as in the great conflict now being waged against medievalism—positives thereby are advanced, negatives banished, and earth's consciousness brought nearer to recognition of its essential oneness.

"The world should recognize sudden death as a great tragedy, yet don't cause people to think that its horror lasts; the glory of my freedom dawns quickly."

There was opportunity now for me to ask my question, "How can the war result in a waste of consciousness if those killed survive, as you assure us?"

"Undeveloped quantity," Stephen replied. "You will understand this later."

Another long pause—then, "I have a new experience for you."

Perhaps the spelling that came next impressed us so greatly because of the contrast it offered to the realism of what had gone before.

"A poet is here," Stephen was saying. "He wishes to attempt a sonnet, in the Italian form. The sonnet is written by one poet to another."

It was the first time any one other than Stephen had come to our ouija-board; the professor was not to appear until three or four weeks later.

The presence of the stranger was evidenced by a new technic, if I may use the word. The tripod's movements were deliberate, whereas Stephen's spellings, after our first experience at Mrs. Jevon's, had become brisk. Here is what the tripod spelled:

"Hail, singing soul that loved so greatly well!
Now art thou come, rose-crowned and radiant,
To keep that most triumphant sacrament Of light,
　more light; while choiring voices swell
　In chants of welcome, as glad minster bell
Acclaims a princely birth of wide portent.
March on, brave poet soldier!
Thy extent Of vict'ry shall earth's visionings excel.

"There is no death! Life is but prophecy,
And burneth on through thine own love's desire
For love supreme. And as thy youth, impearled
In rhyme, is treasure of time's memory,
So, too, shalt thou, whose beauties did inspire
Such fame, sing on in this sublimer world."

When the lines were completed—despite the tripod's air of deliberateness they came in an incredibly short time, more quickly, I fancy, than earthly poets are accustomed to turn even doggerel rhymes—Stephen announced his presence and asked if Joan could tell to whom the poem was indited.

"To Rupert Brooke, of course," she answered.

"Right," said Stephen.

"It was a great honor that was paid you, for you must know that the sonnet's author has graduated close toward the supreme. He is far beyond my degree and that of you two not unsympathetic materialists."

When Mrs. K. read this sonnet—it was shown her on the occasion of her visit — her first question was, "Did either of you ever write poetry?"

Doubtless if we did the performance would be of no evidential worth. It was so pronounced, for Joan has written verse. Who hasn't? But Joan's verse has been born in much travail. The ouija-board sonnet, whatever its value as poetry, sprang into spontaneous being; this at the time impressed Joan and me deeply. And, while we do not wish to insist on the evidential value of the performance, we believe, in view of the later experiment at the piano, that, granted the dead do survive and can or would communicate with the living, communication of verse would be successful only if the receiving station himself had the poetic sense.

At all events, the ease with which the sonnet was written remains most astounding. Note how it draws on two of Brooke's poems, "The Great Lover" and "The Hill." In "The Hill" Brooke speaks of going down "with unreluctant tread rose-crowned into the darkness," and finds comfort in the thought that despite death "life burns on through other lovers, other lips"; note how the ouija-board sonnet turns the latter phrase to a new meaning. The tripod's ready adaptation of Brooke's phrases is interesting in itself, familiar though these phrases were to Joan. That the adaptations should have been woven into an original poem, without apparent effort on Joan's part, seemed and still seems an astonishing thing.

"Brooke," spelled Stephen, "was given a royal welcome when he came here."

"He was satisfied to die?" asked Joan. "His life promised much."

"A supremely great poet," answered Stephen, "once spoke of our land as the country from which no traveler returns. Those who have traveled hither would not return. We never look backward. The tree goes up toward the light, and the sunflower turns its face toward the glory of the morning. And so we here lift our souls up toward the supreme."

"But, Stephen," I said," do you realize that the thought of talking to the soul of a dead man gets a fellow's goat? Do you understand my slang?"

"Perfectly," he replied. "You know it was my slang, too, not so long ago. And in answer to your question let me say I do realize how weird the experience is to you. Had I had a similar experience when I was on the earthplane, I would have considered it wild-eyed and batty. There is a verse in the Psalms that runs something like this— 'He shall give his angels charge over thee lest thou dash thy foot against a stone.' This promise is often quoted for the comforting of men. But the instant it becomes a known reality, hysterics ensue. As for you two, whatever may be your convictions or doubts, you entertain both without hysteria. It is a hopeful sign that others in the unsettled world can be taught the great dignity of living."

"What do you mean by the word 'unsettled'?" Joan asked.

"Those who in sorrow have no light," Stephen spelled. "You cannot realize the modern tragedy that is the result of the past years of skepticism."

"But weren't you skeptical when you were here?" I queried.

"Yes," he answered, "and it is my realization of the simplicity and beauty of the truth that makes me want to teach it to you."

At this point a leg of the ouija-board's tripod became loosened and went bounding over the floor. I followed it down and set about making hasty repairs. Yet so interested were both Joan and I in the words Stephen had been spelling that, though the mending proceeded, we gave it scarcely a thought. Therefore, we were slow of understanding when our fluent speller, privileged at last to resume his discourse, announced, "Joan, Darby was using it for a rest and holding up the procession."

"Using what for a rest?" I asked.

"That silly flatiron thing. Get me?" answered Stephen, again betraying a familiarity with slang quite equal to my own.

"Well, you see, Stephen," I said, "Joan and I discussed you last night until three in the morning."

"Well," spelled Stephen, "I did not ask you to make a circus of yourselves, did I?"

Imagine such a remark from out the great beyond!

"Stephen," said I, "in addition to instructing Joan and me you amuse us."

And Stephen made me an answer which I think pierces deep. He said, "I laugh yet."

Now I had always supposed that, whatever immortality death might hold for thought and serious endeavor, laughter, at least, died here. The earthly trappings of death, black for the mourner's eye and dirges for his ear, have lent their somberness to whatever of victory we have sensed beyond the grave. And yet how victorious is laughter! We are accustomed to deify and call chief attributes of God those characteristics that distinguish man from lower forms of life—consecutive thought, moral responsibility. And is not a sense of humor one of the graces accorded man and denied all lesser being? May not it, too, be divine? Somehow I am happy to know that Stephen, if he be Stephen, still laughs.

XVIII

CONSCIOUSNESS, THE REALITY

WE did not talk with Stephen again for more than a week; Joan and I spent the holidays away from home. I was eager, during the entire time, to be back, so that we might continue our ouija-board conversations. But Joan, I noted, seemed to be losing interest. I asked her why.

"Well," she said, "the philosophy is quite remarkable, of course. But where does it lead to? So much theorizing without a practical end in sight! I'll tell you, Darby: If when we die, we don't—why, that's just a fact. If it's fact, it can be allowed to take care of itself."

"But," said the Adam in me, "it was you who were curious about 'quality of conscious

"But I'm not," she answered, "not unless it gets me somewhere. As far as life after death is concerned, if there is such a thing, we'll know all about it soon enough—we need only wait."

Nonetheless when we got home Joan brought the ouija-board from its hiding-place behind the trunk.

"Hello, people!" was Stephen's greeting. "Shall we go on with the discussion?"

"The discussion" evidently meant "the revelation." We told Stephen to proceed.

"Well, then," the tripod spelled, "I have said that consciousness is. It is the one and only reality. Now, consciousness has many attributes, two of which are so basic that all others are servants to them. Reason, will, matter—these and a host of other attributes are servants to the two fundamentals I have already spoken of—quality and quantity."

"Define the quality and quantity of consciousness," I said.

Stephen answered: "Quality is soul, as when you say a person has a beautiful or sensitive soul. Soul is the best word for our present purpose, though character would in a measure express the thought. I have told you that graduated consciousness is, in part, reborn into your world. I tell you now that the part so reborn is the quality, the soul."

"Your definition," I said, "is not as opaque as a brick wall, nor is it as clear as a windowpane."

"Later the thought will shape itself," Stephen assured me. "And now for quantity. Quantity is that development which results from the use an individual makes of his quality of consciousness."

"Do you mean growth of character?" asked Joan.

"Exactly," Stephen replied. "My renewed reference to the quality and quantity of consciousness is not for the purpose of making the terms wholly understandable to you at this time; I wish simply to keep them before you. Suppose now, Darby, you tell me what you understand by consciousness."

I said, "Consciousness is awareness of self."

"Well, yes," Stephen half assented; and added, "It is in degrees."

Recalling a phrase from the old French philosopher, I remarked: "As Descartes said, 'I think; therefore I am.' By the way, Stephen, do you know the philosophy of Descartes?"

"Not very well," he answered. "... Descartes would hold now that consciousness is more than thought. In the same way an insect, if you could interview the thing, would tell you that consciousness is less than thought. Listen! Consciousness is. It is the all. It is the one and only reality, though its degrees and the attributes thereof are many. Without suggestion from me evolution should indicate to you that the degrees are not fixed.

Out of the lower, remember, the higher; out of the simple, the complex."

Suddenly, as though by a burst of light, my understanding was illumined. Even as Stephen spoke there was answered for me the earth-old riddle—what is reality?

At this point I wish to outline the metaphysical equipment I brought to the ouija-board. This digression is not necessitated by possibility of my subliminal authorship of the Stephen philosophy. The subconscious theory of psychic communication would absolutely demand examination of Joan's metaphysical interest, had she possessed either philosophic bent or knowledge; but no such demand is made in my own case. The reason for intruding my pre-Stephen thought lies simply in the chance that it may offer others, as it offered me, an approach to Stephen's viewpoint.

Some years ago, in a certain Western university, I took a brief course in philosophy, from which I learned only the asking of a riddle, What is the basic reality?

I found myself soon inclined to reject the so-called common-sense, or dualistic, answer, which says: "The material world is real; so is the spiritual. Reality is twofold." To me it seemed that reality could not be other than one. Therefore, I was attracted to monism, of whatever stripe.

Under the influence of idealistic monists—a Bishop Berkeley, for instance—I said: "Matter is a mere combination of properties. Place a pinch of sugar in a man's hand. Through the medium of his senses he will identify it. But let the man become blind; no longer can he identify the sugar by its color. Let him also lose his sense of taste, next his sense of smell, now his touch, and finally his hearing. It is apparent that for the man so bereft the sugar has ceased to exist. If, then, in all the universe there were no mind to perceive, there could be nothing to be perceived. Matter has no reality outside the mind."

Then under the influence of materialistic monists—Haeckel and other exponents of science— I said: "Thought is a function of the material brain. Mind, spirit, is but a property of matter. Matter is the only reality."

Next I connected with the seeming sanity of Kant. Under his influence I said: "Berkeley is right when he asserts that all the mind knows of external objects is its own sense perceptions of them and the resulting ideas. But from this it does not follow that the external world in and of itself is other than real. Mind is real; so also is the thing-in-itself of matter. But what that thing-in-itself is, mind, knowing perceptions only, cannot determine."

The sanity of Kant was attractive, but in the end the hopeless skepticism of his position repelled me. And so I sought for a *tertium quid*, a third something, a fundamental of which mind and matter were mere expressions. Under the influence of Schopenhauer I said, "Will is the only real, appearing in one activity as mind, and in another as material force."

And thus I was accustomed to find my one reality to-day in mind and to-morrow in matter, though feeling all the while that somehow total rejection of dualism was as close to error as its acceptance. And the next day I found reality in "will-to-live," only to reject it the day following; I could not bring myself to believe with the arch-pessimist that life is but blind, purposeless struggle, whose proper ideal is an automaton.

And then finally the riddle I could not solve ceased to interest me. I closed the chapter, five years before the coming of Stephen, by saying: "Doubtless there is but one reality. Science would suggest that it is a colossal, absorbing force of which matter and its energies constitute one phase, and life another. It is neither of these fundamentally. What it is, in a final analysis, is beyond determination. A skepticism wider even than Kant's is justified, with but one offsetting hope—evolution, which, however, to the individual promises nothing. As for personal immortality, that is beyond the bounds of the possible. Individuality is but a tarrying on the way to union with the unknown and unknowable One."

Mrs. K., I think, came to Joan and me beset by a somewhat similar belief, whether or no she reached it by the route I had traveled. Her grief, however, was causing her to seek a way out. I, at the time of Stephen's coming, was five years removed from any wish to circumvent my conclusions. For five years I had not read a single work directly touching on metaphysics; indeed, the once attractive riddle had become unattractive, seldom occurring to my thought save as an occasional "fallen man" sermon might stir me to protest the church's ignoring of evolution, my one ray of light.

And yet all the while I knew that I was real. And in a way I had analyzed my own reality. In myself I recognized two selves, the self that thinks, that wills, that does, and that other self—the sitter-behind and looker-on. Just as I might see Joan turn the leaves of a book, so I saw myself seeing her. I spoke always of *my* thought, *my* will, *my* act. The thinker, the wilier, the doer of *me* was quite as much under my own observation as under Joan's.

"Consciousness is," Stephen spelled that night following the holidays. "It is the one and only reality, though its degrees and the attributes thereof are many."

Attributes? Why, of course! The so-to speak self that thinks, that wills, that does, is but an aggregate of attributes that belong to that other self, that sitter-behind and looker on, in short the me of me, consciousness.

How simple it is! Where else should we look for reality except in the only thing that is truly real to us? Our senses may deceive us; we may doubt them. Our reason is altogether fallible, reaching conclusions which later are shown to be false. Our will may lead us aright or astray. All of these we can doubt, do doubt. Man doubts all things except the fact of his own being, his own consciousness.

But, even so, I would not have fully understood Stephen save for his word "degree."

"Does it follow that because man's only reality is his own consciousness that consciousness is the all?" I asked the ouija-board.

"But," answered Stephen, "consciousness is in degrees. The individual consciousnesses which you associate with what you call life constitute but the higher earth-plane degrees, study of which, from the lowest degree to man, has produced the theory of natural evolution. Must it not be that life evolved from degrees lower than its own? The sting of this thought will be gone once men know that my development here is a parallel to natural evolution, that I am a combination of life quite as they know it, governed by laws that parallel the natural world—I am tempted to say, by the same laws in a higher and more potentially refined form.

"Listen! The supreme degree of consciousness is no different in kind from the consciousness that is within me, and that which is within me is no different in kind from the consciousness that is within you. There is no difference in kind between the consciousness within you and that within the bat, between the consciousness within the bat and that within the weed. And the consciousness of the weed is no different in kind from that which manifests itself as an electrical current, and the consciousness manifested by the electrical current is no different in kind from that which manifests itself as what you call inanimate, inorganic matter. Consciousness is. It is the one and only reality, alike always in kind, though its degrees are many."

Joan stirred uneasily. "But suppose all that you say is true," she protested. "How will it help me to live?"

"Be patient, Joan," spelled the tripod, and, ignoring Joan's question, continued: "Your men of the books and laboratories, once they become monists, all seek to find a fundamental in their favorite attribute of reality. The idealist has made mind supreme, denying the existence of matter; and the materialist has made matter supreme, denying the existence of mind; whereas the truth is that both mind and matter are real, though not dualistically so. Both are attributes of one that is a greater than either. Other thinkers, realizing that somewhere in the backward of things living there is a reality more fundamental than mind, a reality that links matter and spirit in an evolutionary chain, probe deep; yet, like the idealists and materialists, they, too, have been content with a mere attribute—a primitive attribute, such as will, yet only an attribute.

"Listen! Consciousness is all there ever was, is, or will be forever, for consciousness is time."

XIX

QUALM

"THE qual-i—pzg-c-o—"

Stephen of the ouija-board, having discussed consciousness so eloquently, went a lumbering gait when next Joan and I conjured him. Laboriously the tripod moved from letter to letter, became incoherent, then stopped dead.

Long we sat, but Stephen came not. "And," Joan sighed, "I thought everything would go so smoothly this evening."

"Why more smoothly than before?" said I.

"Well," she answered, "I was rummaging about to-day, and I found a can of that woodwork wax the painters used when they did over the dining-room. I thought that if the ouija-board were polished it would work better. So I waxed it."

"Great business!" I said. "The wax has gummed up the felt tips of the tripod's legs."

With turpentine I removed the lily's paint, and again we placed our hands upon the tripod. Behold! Our lost friend was found.

"At least," spelled Stephen, "my legs are not bandied any more."

"What can he mean by that?" I exclaimed.

"You remember one of the pointer's legs came out the other night," Joan laughed. "While I was at the waxing I glued Stephen's, I mean the tripod's, legs in."

"Thanks, Joan," spelled the tripod.

"And now," Stephen continued, "let us go on with the discussion. Our subject to-night is the quality of consciousness. Quality of consciousness, as I have already told you, is the soul. But do not understand by the word 'soul' the entire content of the word 'consciousness.' Consciousness is not merely qualitative; it is quantitative as well."

"Then," said I, "there is possible a qualitative and quantitative analysis of consciousness, like that chemistry has made of matter?"

"What you call matter is but the form attribute of consciousness," Stephen replied. "If chemists have found certain materially manifested degrees subject to qualitative and quantitative analysis, is it not time the psychologists were similarly analyzing the spiritually manifested degree— human consciousness?"

It was, indeed, high time, I supposed. But somehow my mind had strayed from quality and quantity and gone back to consciousness itself. Consciousness as the one reality, which coincidentally with Stephen's explanation had seemed so clear, now had become hazy.

"Stephen," I said, "you contend that consciousness is the all. Really, an inanimate object doesn't appear to possess consciousness in any degree whatsoever."

"But neither do many forms of life itself," came back Stephen. "In fact, you don't know so very much about the consciousness of your fellow-men. Believe me, some of them have darn little."

The thoroughgoingness both of Stephen's language and of his insight into human character brought to Joan's face and mine a smile.

"Stephen," said I, "would it be possible for me to accept the truth of this revelation, so called by you, and at the same time hold that in you as a personality distinct from Joan and me there is no truth?"

"Why," answered the ouija-board, "I suppose so, if your mind be that nimble."

At this still deeper thrust into mortal frailty Joan and I laughed outright.

"You do amuse us, Stephen," I said.

"Well, bear in mind," he answered, "that we are not long-faced here. We have no regrets, therefore no sorrow."

"Why," I offered, "I take it for granted that this earth drama is watched by you graduated ones from your up-yon gallery. If, then, Stephen, you saw an earth friend in trouble, would you not feel sorry for him?"

"You put it strongly," he replied. "And yet I answer, no. For sorrow—that is, real sorrow, as distinct from worry—is a hallucination."

"Do you mean to say that if a man here is ill and penniless, and if his children are hungry and crying for bread, and if there is no bread, do you mean to say that that is not real sorrow?"

"Such things need not be," spelled Stephen.

"But such things are," spoke up practical Joan.

"Do not misunderstand me," replied Stephen. "Many unhappy things are on earth, many things that are negative. When consciousness is fully developed these things will not be." A pause, then, "Do you know that as I stand here watching you as I once was—"

Joan started out of her chair, and the entire ouija outfit went crashing to the floor. "Standing where watching!" she cried.

"Frightened, Joan?" I asked, gathering up my scattered notes. She seated herself again. A moment of waiting, and then—

"Dear woman," the invisible Stephen spelled, "I did not mean to startle you, but this is not the first time I have spoken of my materiality. You know, the world knows, that space is full of sights and sounds beyond the human eye and ear. Let us go on. But first, Joan, promise me that you will continue to talk with me until I have told you all the 'philosophy,' as Darby calls it."

The tripod had moved rapidly; I withdrew both hands in order to bring my notes down to date.

"I won't promise a piece of wood anything," rebelled Joan.

Yet when I jokingly accused her of being interested only in having her fortune told, she said, "Come on." Again we placed our hands upon the tripod.

"Why should I seek to tell fortunes," queried Stephen, "since you two and I are playing such wonderful parts in the great drama of consciousness? Listen! Could there be a greater thing than pointing the way to scientists, to biologists, chemists, philosophers, for the constructing of a reasonable proof that man's idea of death is wrong, that it is an idea only, not a fact? You pin your faith to your laboratories these days, and that is well; man has all truth within his grasp. All he needs is a light, a clear guide for the separation of facts from emotional hypotheses. Do not be a foolish virgin, Joan. You are the lamp, but I am the oil, and a lamp without oil can give no light."

"Stephen means," I expounded, "that his philosophy is like studying Greek, which is brainfagging till you learn it. Then a wonderful literature is yours."

"Or like an automobile, I suppose," said Joan, "a joyous, breeze-creating thing on a hot night, but made possible by the dust and heat of shops and the sweat of many hands."

"But surely," spelled Stephen. "The truth I tell, when so linked with modern scientific fact that reasoning minds can accept it, will be a joyous, breeze-creating thing. It will bring coolness to hearts hot with sorrow. It will tell my mother that life and happiness and a chance of making good are not ended for me. And that's what she's crying over; that's all that the mothers and wives are crying over—the thought that we are giving our lives before we had our chance. I would tell them that he that loses his life shall find it. For 'there is no death—life is but prophecy'! But let us go on with our discussion of quality.

"When I speak of the quality of gold as being distinct from the quality of iron, the word presents no difficulty. Yet when I speak of the quality of human consciousness you are confused. This should not be, but—as Joan might say—because it is, I tell you the quality of a man's consciousness is his soul.

"Take electricity. It is force. Take gravitation. It, too, is force. Now the thing that distinguishes these two forces one from the other is their differing quality.

"Well, the quality of human consciousness is parallel to the quality of gravitation and to the quality of electricity. The earth term heretofore used for the quality of human consciousness has been soul, by which term men have sought to name that which distinguishes them from all else.

In other words, they have recognized the distinctiveness of their own quality."

"Why, that's simple enough," I was forced to admit.

"And all great truths are most astounding in their simplicity," spelled the ouija-board.

"And now let us say," Stephen continued, "that a child is born into your world. The quality of that child's consciousness consists of a given degree of soul endowment, fixed at birth. The quality of the child's consciousness, the quality of your consciousness and that of all individuals, is, on the earth-plane, unalterable. Fixed at birth, it can in earth-life neither be heightened nor lowered.

"It is all so plain, when related up to lives as you observe them. Take, for instance, your own impulses, and compare them with those of a criminal. You could not commit murder; such is your quality of consciousness. Yet the real murderer, as distinct from the man who is drunk or angered or insane, actually plans his crime. Such is his quality. These instincts . . . are the visible indications of quality. Educate the potential murderer all you will, the instinct will not change, though the deed may, in fact, never be committed."

A fatalistic view, you say. So said Joan and I, and so we insisted until we understood more clearly. It was one of the wonders of the ouija-board's discourse that fuller understanding did always come.

Once Stephen referred to his discussion as an "all-explanatory philosophy."

"Why," said I, "has the mere fact of graduation made you omniscient?"

"No," he answered, "but the truth of this revelation applied to all earth theories of any dignity will differentiate between the fundamental facts and the emotional hypotheses."

And such, in fact, has been my experience and Joan's. This and that hoary dogma, long realized by us to be false, still for some unknown reason would exercise a spell over us. Suddenly by the magic of Stephen's philosophy the spell is lifted, also accounted for. In these dogmas we have recognized, thanks to Stephen, an ounce of truth embedded in a pound of error. Let me illustrate.

The doctrine of fatalism, asserting that man is helpless quite in the grip of predetermined destiny, has constituted the keystone of many a religion's arch. Even in Christian thought, a system essentially optimistic, Calvinistic predestination, foreordaining some to be saved and some to be damned, has found lodgment. Fatalism has refused to down.

Why? Because there is in the thought a glimpse, a fundamental fact; to wit, that the quality of consciousness, supernature's gift to the natural plane, cannot on earth be altered by a jot or a tittle. And no fatalism is involved here. "For," says Stephen, "quantitatively men are free. Quantity is developed on your plane. Use to the utmost the quality my plane has vouchsafed you."

"By the way," I interjected, "this rebirth of quality, Stephen—that's a thing which has been puzzling me. It is mystical, to say the least."

"Nothing is mystical," spelled the ouija-board. "I cite you one of man's primest emotional hypotheses: The human mind enjoys a mystery. Rebirth offers a mystery at least no greater than birth itself. Think it over."

Now all the while Joan had, indeed, been thinking. For the sake of clearness I elaborate her question as follows:

"Stephen, you say that the quality of an individual's consciousness is unalterable on the earth-plane. You say that the qualities of the inanimate world are likewise unalterable. There on the table lies a book. Color is a noticeable quality of that book's binding. The color is red. Stephen, I can dip that binding into various dyes and at will make it green, blue, any color I choose. Where now is the unalterableness of quality?"

"Tut, tut!" Stephen returned. "You should seek your parallel not in a compound such as a book. Human consciousness is not compounded. It is an elemental thing. Color is not the essential quality of the book, or of the binding. If the binding were black it would still be a binding and the book a book. By the word quality I refer to essential quality; to that quality, for example, which makes the book a book rather than a glass of water.

"Take electricity again. Can you not see that its quality is fixed? It is that very unalterableness of quality that makes it electricity rather than, for example, centrifugal force. So it is with human consciousness. But now get this: Though your quality on the earth-plane is restricted, I on my plane am free to develop quality, just as you now are free to develop quantity."

The tripod paused, then moved, then halted again, then said: "Does it mean anything to you when I say that the only difference between your plane of consciousness and mine is that yours is quantitative in its development, while mine is qualitative? At any rate, from now on I shall speak of my plane as the qualitative plane and yours as the quantitative. And now will you please ask questions?"

Joan, the practical, wanted to know how the individual in this world can turn the quality of his consciousness to individual advancement. And I, whom Stephen has accused of "seeking to read metaphysics into the grass underfoot," wanted to know how quality is developed in the world beyond.

"Let us dispose of the qualitative plane first," spelled Stephen. "It is apparent that for man quality development is a new thought. Therefore, there are no earth terms by which I can adequately describe the process. The best I can do is to tell you some facts.

"For one thing, we here associate with degrees higher than ourselves, and learn from them. Of course, our perceptions, our understanding, all our attributes, are intensified, and the knowledge that became ours upon graduation makes us eager to avail ourselves of all opportunities.

"For another thing, we serve. Having learned the oneness of consciousness, we seek to aid the development of degrees lower than ourselves. Of my service on the battle-fields I have already told you.

"Truth to tell, we here are, on the one hand, development, and, on the other hand, we are service."

"But," I asked, "aren't there any slackers there?"

"No," answered Stephen. "All who are here want to do all they can. But, of course, those who graduated from the primary grades of earth cannot immediately enter college—I use the expression figuratively, yet not so figuratively, after all. Joan, ask your questions concerning quality on earth."

"Well," said she, "there are so many people in life who seem capable of much, yet accomplish little. I have met many a poet who never wrote a line and farmers who never turned a furrow. Yet always these persons believe they could, if they would, and that conviction is often shared by those who best know them. The poemless poets and the fieldless farmers are an unhappy set, I have noticed, discounting their successes as carpenters and bankers. Has the individual quality of consciousness anything to do with this bit of unhappiness?"

"But surely," spelled Stephen, "though I must ask you not to confuse quality and talent. Men of the same quality frequently have diverse talents; the same quality might find satisfactory expression in finance, in agriculture. But of the man who forever is dissatisfied with what his hand and brain find to do I would say this: He has refused to listen to the voice of his quality."

"Let us see," said Joan. "Do you mean that a John Keats could happily conduct a cigar store?"

"I have not said so," Stephen replied. "But take from a John Keats the talent of verse writing and substitute the music talent. Can you not see that his quality would have been just as satisfactorily fulfilled? Keats's father kept a livery stable. Had the son submitted to the fate that pointed out for him the life of a groom, he would have stifled his quality. After all, you can't use a silk purse as a sow's ear."

"Why," asked Joan, as we laughed at Stephen's reversal of the proverb, "do we believe in the silk purse even when we see it used as a sow's ear?"

"The world has always recognized high quality," answered Stephen, "even when the individual possessing it refuses to develop quantity. It is the soul that counts."

"But can't quality retrograde? If not here, then in your world?" asked Joan.

The tripod almost leaped from under our fingers.

"Never!" shouted our marvelous ouija-board. "Never!"

And what a thought is there! Old, doubtless. Most truths, Stephen assures us, have been glimpsed. Yet to us, accustomed as men and women are to seeing conscience overruled, promise unfulfilled, development throttled, the thought seemed new.

"Joan," I cried, "the quality of consciousness, the soul of us, cannot go backward, cannot be damned. What of quality the consciousness that is within us has won through ages of development is truly won, beyond peril of slipping down again into its low past. Its dreams may, for the now, go unrealized; its promptings may be heard only to be ignored; yet it will ever prompt and ever dream."

"It's up to you to follow it," spelled the tripod. "The voice of a man's quality is his one sure guide. Listen to that voice, then follow it wherever it leads, and in the going you will best be serving not only yourself, but the great whole of which you are a part."

The old quotation came involuntarily to my lips:

This above all: To thine own self be true,
And it must follow, as the night the day,
Thou canst not then be false to any man.

"A true glimpse," spelled Stephen.

XX

THE PROFESSOR

QUANTITY of consciousness, according to Stephen, is developed through the use will makes of the quality of consciousness.

This statement, as I thought it over, seemed to introduce a new element, and so I asked, "Where does will come from?"

"Will," Stephen answered, "is simply freedom for individual development. True, man's free will parallels certain aspects of instinct and even of organic and inorganic reaction. Yet between these extremes of a thing alike throughout in kind there is a difference of—" In the midst of the sentence Joan withdrew her hands from the tripod. "I am tired of theories," she said. "I wish Stephen would get some one to give us another sonnet."

"All right, ask him!" I agreed, eager for a test of the ouija-board's ability to duplicate its previous poetical performance.

"Why, yes, if you like," the board spelled. "There was once a poet who committed suicide. He has been wanting to talk—everybody here wants to talk. It's quite as unusual for us as for you, you know. The poet will be here in a minute; I've called him. While we are waiting, Joan, just let me say this: Quantity of consciousness is the gift the individual makes to the whole. Here's the poet."

Then, without hesitating, save at the end of each line, that I might write the words down, the ouija-board spelled the following:

"From wakening sun till sleeping star, my race
Was but a feeble span of flickering light—
A lonely candle casting through the night
But shadow's shadow on the wavering face
Of men's emotions, then puffed out apace.
Oh, earth-contorted concepts and the blight
Of truths but glimpsed, your soul-benumbing
might
Now sweeps o'er nations like a flaming mace!
"And I, whose own hand rent the temple veil,
Essaying entrance bare of preciousness
That wise men offer, now say this to thee:
Regret is vain; for rust cannot empale
The quality of gold, and consciousness
Sits judge of self and her free-willed degree."

With the sonnet completed and recorded in my note-book, Joan asked, as we placed our fingers back on the tripod, "Is the poet still here?"

"Yes," spelled the board. "Have you been a long time dead?" asked Joan.

"I have been here a long time," the tripod answered. "It would seem so to you. But we do not count time as you do."

"Have you been happy?"

"Very happy, as are all who are here," was the reply. "My only regret, which is useless, is that I played the Judas to my quality, that I failed to contribute to the common whole of my degree here the gift of quantity. The potentiality of my quality would have made it possible for me to have offered something not unworthy."

165

"Perhaps," said Joan, "you left the world poems that it still finds beautiful?"

"That men's thoughts," the ouija-board spelled, "live after them in the memory of those who await graduation, is one of the greatest of all glimpses. For that intellect so strong as to produce of itself thoughts and words that survive it must of necessity be more potential than its production."

"Have you since your death ever before talked to any one here on earth?" questioned Joan.

"Not directly," came the answer. "This is my first privilege."

"And how do you busy yourself?" Joan next asked. "Does one go on writing poetry for

"What we strive for here," the poet replied, "is the height of consciousness, the perfect realization of individuality and of that individuality's relation to the whole. And now, good-by!"

The tripod resumed its customary bobbing speed, and we knew that Stephen was again "on the line."

"I think," said he, "that the sonnet just given you exquisitely illustrates the idea of quality and quantity. First the poet tells you of his quality, the nickering light which could burn but faintly in a world of emotional hypotheses. Then he recalls to your mind the great war, in its inception the supreme egotism of the ages. But even in thought so overwhelming he cannot forget his own personally supreme emotional hypothesis, his suicide. Thereby he halted his development of quantity. Yet how beautifully he puts the glorious truth: 'Rust cannot empale the quality of gold. Equally glorious is the truth he states in conclusion, that consciousness, free-willed in its higher degrees, is judge of self. And now, here is some one else who would like to talk to you."

The some one was—the professor. It was his first appearance.

"This, my dear sir and madam, is Professor X.," the tripod spelled. "The poem just dictated to you, and that dictated some time ago, are truly wonderful demonstrations of the possibilities of communication between the two planes. These demonstrations are a very great satisfaction to me. But in your enthusiasm for the beauties of poesy do not neglect the more important phase of the revelation, the literal statement of truth."

Here was the professor saying outright, I am So-and-so. The anomaly of the pointblank statement was not apparent to me at the time, because I knew nothing of coloring. But when Stephen later explained how readily the subconscious mind of a receiving station can distort a name or other concrete item of fact, Joan and I asked ourselves what assurance there could be that the communicator claiming to be Professor X. really was he, if, indeed, there was involved anything other than an obscure phenomenon of our own mentality.

It was with this question in mind that I read Mrs. K., on the occasion of her visit with us, a number of the communications we had received from the professor. She was interested, it will be remembered, by the suggestion of agreement between the personality of our professor and that of the actual professor, though she indicated she did not know Professor X. intimately enough to justify her in expressing a really definite opinion.

Interrupting briefly the narrative of Stephen's philosophy, I shall here relate certain messages that came shortly after Mrs. K.'s visit. To Joan and me they seem pertinent to the question: Was our professor really So-and-so?

On April 10, 1919, I asked, in the course of mental communication, "Is there any message for Mrs. K?"

The response was introduced by the name "Helen," three times repeated. Then the communicator, whom at the time we supposed to be Mr. K., appeared to be showing Joan the interior of a house, first a library, then an up-stairs room, and finally a hall. Joan, speaking in her own character, sought to describe this interior. When the communication was finished I touched Joan's wrist, and read her my notes. We agreed that the message was intended for Mrs. K., if for any one. And so the script was forwarded her with this statement: "'Helen' is a new name so far as we are concerned. It has never appeared before, and means nothing to us."

Then on April 13th, before sufficient time had elapsed for receipt of a reply from Mrs. K., the professor appeared, saying:

"I have put it over at last, my dear sir, put it over at last."

"Why, good evening, professor," I said, recognizing the customary form of address— "my dear sir."

And then the professor surprised me by speaking the name "Helen." He followed the name with: "My dear Mrs. K., do not be afraid to cross the bridge. ... If it would not be too much trouble for you, cross the bridge. . . . Tell Helen you have crossed the bridge." He paused, then said: "Not forgotten the promise, promise I made to manifest myself from totally unheard-of quarter, Helen. . . . After years this is answer, Helen. Tried hard for two years here. . . . Put it over, by George! put it over. . . . Boats, boats on the river. Rowboats."

Studying this communication of April 13th, Joan and I wondered whether we had not jumped at conclusions when we associated the communication of April 10th with Mr. K. Could the April 10th communicator have been the professor? Was the name of our professor's wife Helen? Mrs. K. would know. A copy of the April 13th communication was sent her.

A letter from Mrs. K., received about a week later, commented on both the April 10th communication and that of the 13th. She said: "When I read the first Helen script it had no significance for me. Then I thought of the wife of your professor. Her name is Helen."

Mrs. K. went on to say that she had showed the two scripts to the professor's wife, who had found them interesting. Why? I submit the facts of the case with little comment, other than to say that Joan—or I, if knowledge of mine could matter one way or the other—knew practically nothing of Professor X.'s personal life.

The interior description, linked as it was with the coming of the name "Helen," proved rather impressive; for, despite vagueness and certain inaccuracies, the house described might, it seemed, be the X. home.

For instance, Joan's description of the library made reference to a "long, long table." The professor's library, we learned from Mrs. X., who herself wrote us finally relative to the communications, did contain a very long table, made originally for some one who wanted to spread engravings out on it. On the other hand, the communication's effort to specify the table's position with reference to the bookshelves of the room was a failure. Other details of the library, as described in the communication, were hardly more successful, except one—reference to a student-lamp.

A sentence of the library description was: "He" (by which, I took it, Joan meant the "Helen" communicator) "says he had a Student-lamp and the cussed thing smoked."

In Joan's experience, oil as an illuminant has been supplanted by electricity. What would prompt her subliminal to guess that Professor X. preferred to remain faithful, in his library, to the "student-lamp" of his earlier years? If guess it was, it hit home with astonishing accuracy.

"My husband read preferably by a student lamp," Mrs. X. wrote us. "He would often turn it too high and then be disgusted if the 'wretched thing' smoked. He might or might not have called it 'cussed.' The latter expression, however, would easily have translated his annoyance."

The description of the up-stairs room carried mention of a fireplace and "a tall sort of mahogany highboy," and sought to give the location of the fireplace and highboy with reference to various windows. An up-stairs room in the X. home, it proved, does contain a fireplace and also a highboy. But this might be true of any up-stairs room in any home. The communication's attempt to specify the location of the fireplace and highboy, while seeming to approximate accuracy, was not free from confusion. Then, too, the fireplace was described as having "a funny, old-fashioned, curved mouth." The fireplace in the room where the highboy stands does not have a curved mouth. Yet, oddly enough, in another up-stairs room of the X. home, Mrs. X. informed us, there is an old-fashioned fireplace, the mouth of which is curved.

The house interior description closed with Joan's exclaiming: "What a peculiar hall! It hasn't any top. I see; the hall runs clear to the top, with rooms around it on the second floor."

"The reference to the hall is excellent," Mrs. X. said. "The hall does run up two stories, and the rooms on the second floor open off it."

Concerning the house description, viewed as an entirety, Mrs. X. wrote:

"The testimony of each single point is of great interest when a composite picture, as it were, is made. The script conveys an intimate impression of familiarity with the interior of a house unknown to either of you. This is to me the impressive note of the testimony."

Let us pass now to the communication of April 13th. Its item of least interest was the reference to "boats on the river." Professor X. and his wife, it proved, were fond of boating together. But the liking for boating is so general that "boats on the river" would fit the experience of thousands.

Quite curious, however, was the professor's requesting Mrs. K. to "cross the bridge" and to "tell Helen you have crossed the bridge." Was the language simply symbolical? Perhaps so, even if the identity of our professor with Professor X. could be established. Yet the fact is that Mrs. X. lives in a suburb that can be reached from the city proper, where Mrs. K. lives, only by a bridge. Certainly Joan did not know that Mrs. X. lived in this suburb beyond the bridge. Furthermore, Mrs. K. wrote: "It is my impression I told you when I saw you that Mrs. X. was in California. Am I right about this?" She was; indeed, Joan and I had somehow gathered the impression that Mrs. X. had taken up a permanent residence in California.

A further item of interest was contained in the words:

171

"Not forgotten the promise, promise I made to manifest myself from totally unheard-of quarter, Helen. . . . After years this is answer, Helen. Tried hard for two years here. . . . Put it over, by George! put it over."

Mrs. X. wrote us: "It is true that several years ago a sensitive gave me an automatic script purporting to have come from my husband. The message promised that in time, and through an unknown psychic, he would manifest himself to me."

Can it be that all through the two years of our impersonal, philosophic acquaintance with the professor he was eagerly watching for opportunity to send his wife assurance of his being? Had he "put it over at last"?

XXI

INDIVIDUALITY

WHATEVER understanding I possess of Stephen's philosophy came not with sudden fullness that precluded subsequent confusion. Quite the contrary! For instance, while Joan and the poet were hobnobbing, I found time to indulge in no small measure of what Stephen calls hypothetical reasoning. I mobilized my emotions around the word "individual," used by Stephen, just prior to the poet's appearance, in his statement of quantity as the gift of the individual to the whole.

"In the first place," I said, "I don't by any manner of means accept you, Stephen, as an individual outside my own mind and Joan's. If I did, I could not, of course, question the possibility of individualistic survival. But oneness means oneness, Stephen. And oneness ever more perfectly realized seems to be the very heart of your revelation. When the consciousness which is the me of me develops to supremacy, there must then be realized, it would seem, a oneness of myself with the all, so overpowering that my individuality will be quite lost."

"Have you heard my philosophy to so little advantage?" mourned Stephen.

"Listen! The poet has just said: 'What we strive for is the height of consciousness, the perfect realization of individuality and of that individuality's relation to the whole.' The entire story is contained in those words. The supreme degree of consciousness is composed at once of the height of individual consciousness and of the perfection of individual adjustment to the whole."

But old thoughts were still strong upon me. For so long I had scouted hope of personal survival. Try as I might, I was unable to grasp—or, rather, having grasped, hold to— the idea that perfect oneness of the whole and perfect individuality of its parts reasonably can coexist.

Joan is the book-buyer at our house. A day or two after Stephen and I had deadlocked on individuality's survival she saw offered for sale—on a bargain counter, if you please—*A Pluralistic Universe,* by William James.

"I just bought it on a bet," she said, as she handed me the volume.

"And you won," I exclaimed, after I had run through a score of pages. For the elusive thought of oneness joined with many-ness was by the little book made clear.

Here was a monist who, dissatisfied with a oneness which in its ultimate obliterates the many, finally found it reasonable to consider the "each" as fundamental as the "all." The "all," the whole, may be made up, he saw, of a number of parts, or "eaches."

I rushed for the ouija-board and said, "Stephen, are you here?" And, with Joan co-operating, Stephen said, "But, yes."

And then, too filled with my great thought, I— well, I lost it. So, while Joan waited patiently, I took up James's book again, and for a second time skimmed its pages.

Then said I, repossessed of my great new thought, "Stephen, have you gone?"

And Stephen replied, saying: "That is always such an interesting question to answer. If ever I am not present when you call, I shall tell you so."

At this point my notes carry the word "Laughed." We did, I remember—heartily. And then I formulated my thought for Stephen's hearing, something as follows:

"Monism is true. There is but one reality, which, as you say, Stephen, is consciousness. You hold that the high degree of consciousness found in man is the result of millions of years of evolution on this plane and of like ages of development on yours. Further, you link up, through rebirth of quality, quantitative development on earth with qualitative development on your plane, thus spanning the two planes. Now evolution, development, rebirth continue, you say, on and on, with the supreme degree of consciousness as the ultimate. Toward the supreme all consciousness tends; in the end all consciousness, meaning the all of all that is, reaches supremacy. And now, Stephen, your crowning thought is that the ultimate, the supreme, is a perfect whole made up of perfectly adjusted parts. Joan, you, I, all that is, one day will be just such perfect parts, perfectly serving just such a perfect whole. The 'each,' Stephen, is as true a thought as is the 'all.' Individuality endures."

"To hear you speak so," spelled Stephen, "is wonderful. Could you know the satisfaction manifested here! There is joy in heaven, to speak tritely."

"But," I answered, "the credit is not mine. It belongs to James, who wrote the book, and to Joan, who bought the book at a bargain sale."

"No credit to me," said Joan. "I bought the book on impulse, without looking beyond its title—just because the thought flitted through my mind."

"And," said Stephen, "I flitted the thought."

"Pluralistic monism," I mused. "What a phrase! How contradictory, and yet how expressive!"

The failure of religion, I thought, has been that it tends to place God outside the world. Its glory lies in its insistence on the validity of individual experience. The glory of modern speculative science is that, sensing the necessity of the whole, it has sought its deity, its reality, not outside the world, but in it—in energy, in matter, in life. The failure of science is that, having through experimental examination of the parts gained vision of the whole, it straightway deserts experience, permitting its conception of oneness to become a nebulosity. Are not the "each," or part, idea and the "all," or whole, idea inseparably bound together? Is not the apparent contradiction contained in the phrase "pluralistic monism" the veriest logic experience offers?

Addressing Stephen, I said, "I must thank James for the thought contained in that phrase."

The tripod assumed a stately gait. It was our professor. He said: "The phrase 'pluralistic monism' is not James's. It is your own."

"Why, no," I insisted.

"Look in the book," spelled the professor.

I did as he bade me, and, indeed, he was right. Nowhere had James used the phrase. When I returned to the ouija-board I found the professor waiting.

"I knew James well," he said. "His thought was of pluralistic idealism. He had come to realize that oneness, in any true system of logic, could be thought of pluralistically. But, because of the stress the world about him was placing on the modern materialistic interpretation of reality, and because he felt that somehow, despite even science, life did possess a spiritual value, he was veered toward idealism. Had he hit upon the non-committal phrase 'pluralistic monism,' he might have arrived at the exact truth. . . . That he should have missed it by a hair is odd, my dear sir, very odd."

Well, if science should find the one reality in consciousness, let it not feel called upon to miss by a hair the obvious fact that consciousness, however monistic, is in experience pluralistic as well. Consider society. Surely mankind in its social relations tends toward oneness. Surely national development is prophet of that perfect social oneness toward which consciousness strives. Yet nations grow in oneness only as the individual citizens grow toward perfect individuality.

And where now is the emphasis—on oneness or on plurality?

"On oneness, always on oneness," says Stephen. "The height of individuality is but the perfect adjustment of a part to the whole. I am a part of the whole, yet the whole is I. In you, in me, is all that is, consciousness. Yet we are but parts of the greater whole."

I have sought for an illustration that might convey some clear appreciation of pluralistic monism. I offer this:

A fussy audience has gradually filled the music-hall, each individual fussily settling in his seat and fussily waiting for that to happen which brought him and the others together.

At last the orchestra, fifty, seventy-five, one hundred strong, files in upon the stage; and fussily the musicians take their stations. Fussily they tune their instruments and fussily arrange their scores. Then comes the leader. Fussily he bows, fussily faces his players, and taps his baton—perhaps less fussily—in signal for the symphony to begin.

I need not press the figure. You know that the many individuals who compose that orchestra will not cease, during the performance of the symphony, to exist as individuals, that instead they will become more individualistic than ever. Yet, not in spite of that accentuation of individuality, but because of it, the orchestra becomes for the period of the number a whole.

The violins now sigh, now wail. The brass sounds a note of triumph or defeat. The wood pipes gaily or moans mournfully. The drums roll or are silent. And music carries the performers far into the superworld Stephen tells of, a world ever more realized in oneness, ever more perfect in adjustment of the individual to the whole.

And as the music throbs on, a hush falls over that audience of fussy men and women, deepens, broadens, uniting those who play and those who listen into a oneness wherein the parts are so delicately, so rapturously related that surely Stephen is right when he says, "Lay the emphasis on oneness, always on oneness."

XXII

QUANTITY

STEPHEN at our next meeting was wholly ^ determined to complete his discussion of the quantity of consciousness. He led off thus:

"Quantity of consciousness is developed, not simply through the undergoing of mortal experience, but rather through its assimilation. The man who greatly develops his quantity orders his experience, which of itself is chaotic. He learns of life not only knowledge, but wisdom.

"Now, to say that in its potentiality such a servant attribute as reason is qualitative is a fairly accurate way of stating the truth. Its earth-plane development, however, is quantitative. And the individual who develops such an attribute thereby gathers unto himself some measure of quantity, but not necessarily the greatest measure. And why not, Darby?"

"The goal," I answered, "is complete and perfect recognition by the individual of his partness with the whole. Great is the quantity of the man who uses his quality, be it high or not so high, in service of the whole."

"Again," spelled Stephen, "there is joy in heaven. A man of great mental attainment, if he would greatly develop his quantity, must place his mental equipment at the disposal of the whole's development. Truly service is the practical expression of quantity."

And now must I set down the fact that no sooner had my scholarship for a second time caused "joy in heaven," than I betrayed a grievous misunderstanding.

I said: "Except Stephen, as the individual, wins quantity from sources outside himself, from where does it come? And yet how preposterous, if the quantity of one man's consciousness is won by him at the expense of another's!"

"Preposterous is right!" spelled the ouija-board. "I have said nothing to justify your inference. The whole of consciousness can neither increase nor diminish; science has glimpsed this fact in its theory of the conservation of matter and energy. But that whole is subject to development, both of a quantitative and qualitative nature, and the individual differs not from the whole. Man's development on earth is quantitative. This does not mean that he actually amasses consciousness. It means only that that consciousness which he is develops quantitatively. By development of quantity, therefore, I refer to that development which pertains to consciousness as quantity."

I raised the white flag. Joan, complaining of "fine-spun theories," shifted the trend of the discussion.

"Stephen," she said, "can you take a specific individual and tell us of his quantitative development?"

"But surely," answered the ouija-board, inviting Joan and me to consider the instance of one I shall call D. R., an old man afflicted with an incurable disease which, though it permitted him to be about, had rendered him quite childish. Joan and I had spent Christmas with D. R.

"D. R., as you have always recognized, is of a high quality of consciousness," spelled Stephen. "He has, however, developed the quantity of his consciousness out of all proportion to his quality. Though never possessed of great reasoning power, he had an unusually retentive memory. This he developed to its utmost, thereby compensating for what he lacked in reason. Then, too, he had unusual insight into human nature, and this also he fostered. His third great asset was his liking for people and the resulting craving for good opinion. This cast of mind he put to great advantage; it gave him sympathy for many men of many sorts, and at the same time saved him from falling into the pitfalls laid for the good mixer.

"Now, by using what gifts he had, D. R. developed quantity such as is frequently unachieved by men of greater quality. There was, it is true, a selfishness in his quality, but because of his quantitative development he was able to overcome this and give to the world a wonderful service.

"And here is a thought that will bear being kept with you always. D. R., by the development of his own quantity and by virtue of the service that necessarily resulted from that development, was the direct cause of the development of quantity in hundreds of others, the hundreds whom directly and indirectly he served. The thought you will do well always to hold to is this, that the individual's development of the quantity of consciousness leavens the whole of consciousness. 'The kingdom of heaven is like unto leaven, which a woman took and hid in three measures of meal, till the whole was leavened.'"

"Must D. R. soon die?" asked Joan.

"I am no fortune-teller," answered Stephen. "But this I will say, that D. R. is being prepared for graduation. His old friend, H. J." (dead these many years) "is with him constantly. The other day he recognized his friend."

And it was true. A letter we received a few days later told us that D. R. had asked, quite without thought of the thing being abnormal, "What is H. doing here?"

Had D. R., a few months before, mentioned his dead friend as being present with him we would have set the affair down as the hallucination of a wavering mind. Even now we cannot assert that it was otherwise. Yet to be told one week by a ouija-board that D. R. recognized his dead friend's presence, and the next week to be informed in a letter from D. R.'s home that he had inquired, "What is H. doing here?"—this pulls one up to a stop. Can coincidence, the accidental agreement of the words of an irresponsible toy and the actual fact as it was developing miles distant, account for such a happening?

"D. R. will graduate happily," continued Stephen. "His usefulness on earth is impaired by his physical disability, and he is eager for conscious resuming of his work. You may have noticed his restlessness. He is impatient to be away."

"When he has graduated what mind will he have," I asked, "his former active mentality or that which is now his?"

"He is sick now," said Stephen, "that is all. Upon graduation he will come into possession of all that he ever was and far more than he knew himself to be."

"Is, then," Joan asked, "the old-age mind just a sick mind?"

"It results simply from the breaking down of the material brain and nervous system," Stephen replied. "Often, too, as in the case of D. R., old age is a period of preparation for graduation."

"Do you mean that D. R., despite his mental feebleness, is still developing?" I questioned, adding that he seemed so "far away."

"Yes, for graduation," Stephen answered. "That which you note as uncanniness is but the result of new appreciations he is developing, new realization of the whole of which he is a part."

"But," I said, "he seems to me unhappy."

"He is not unhappy," spelled Stephen. "He is but impatient to come back to the whole of his degree of quality, as all who do not experience sudden death are glad to come back. He would come back to the broader consciousness, to recognition of the great truth, to work, to service, and the development of a new quality according to the quantity he has achieved. Already he knows what he always believed, that earth life is preparation of the mortal for immortality."

"Why," I asked, "did he believe this? He never made profession of religion."

"Because in the practice of his calling," Stephen replied, "it was given him to be present at so many graduations and hear the testimony of delight at the meeting of passing souls with friends. It is the beautiful glimpse."

"Death-bed visions?" I asked.

"Yes," said Stephen, "but to the passing soul these experiences are not visions. They are reality."

And then, in seeming defiance of the untheoretical Joan, the ouija-board spelled:

183

"A word more, of summary. Take consciousness as the one and only whole. Suppose it to be divided into halves. Now suppose the individual's consciousness to be divided into halves. The halves of consciousness are quality and quantity. The halves of the individual's consciousness are—at least, for the purpose of psychology—soul and mind. The soul of the individual is to be compared to quality; the mind, to quantity. Now the quality of the consciousness of an individual may be, in fact is, of a certain degree. Degrees of quality may be high or low and are easily recognized; so also it is with quantity. An individual, then, at graduation, possesses his original degree endowment of quality and the added degrees of quantity earth life developed. And just as his development of quantity on earth depended, in the final limit, on his degree of quality, so his qualitative progress here will be governed by his earthly quantitative advance, save, however, as each individual's gift of quantity leavens the whole."

XXIII

DEGREES

MY narrative of the coming of the philosophy has now caught up with and passed Stephen's directing Joan and me to "his record," contained, he had said, in a recently published book. We had, by this time, found the book, its confirmation of the sometime existence of Stephen L startling us into realization that our endeavor to explain the philosophy as some strange expression of my own mind could not ignore Stephen himself.

Granted that somehow I had subconsciously worked out the philosophy and somehow was now releasing it, my subconscious mind could not have fabricated even in guess the definite fact of Stephen L 's earthly existence and the concrete circumstances of his death. But before Stephen had finished his discussion of quantity, such reasoning, so far as my subconscious mind was concerned, had been rendered futile. The spellings, we now knew, came not through me, but Joan; and Joan lacked all knowledge of metaphysics or instinct for it.

It was in the course of this new phase of our bewilderment that Joan's faculty of sensing the letters before they were pointed out on the board developed, with the consequence that her announcement of them was frequently ahead of the tripod. The confusion that resulted was coped with for a while by Joan's keeping silent and my reading the board alone. Then the tripod struck a new gait, deserting its old-time bobbing stride for what, on occasions, was a really furious pace.

Thus handicapped we reached detailed discussion of degrees.

"By degree," spelled the swiftly moving tripod, "is meant that state of consciousness with which a man, or a woman, is born, and with which, subject to development in the mean time through. assimilation of mortal experience, he is graduated."

I asked if a man, despite quantitative development during his earth life, graduated with the same degree of consciousness with which he was born.

"Why, yes," answered Stephen. "But let me illustrate. Take a common field daisy. It will, in its earthly character, always be a daisy, though by cultivation it may be made a tiling of many petals, of intricate life. So it is with the individual."

"Go slower!" I pleaded.

"I shall try to," answered the board. "The receiving station is becoming very practised."

He continued: "The definition of degree I just gave you is, to be sure, a human-value definition. Degrees, however, are as characteristic of all that is as of men and women. Now, because you do not see matter or force in their component parts, it is difficult for you to understand that a stone and electrical energy are manifestations of degrees of the same thing. Yet take carbon. In one form you know it as coal, in another as graphite, and in a third as a diamond. But all the time it is carbon."

"You must go slower," I interjected. "Your speeches have become so long and you reel them off so rapidly!"

"There is not so much need of questions now," Stephen replied. "You are more understanding than you were in the beginning. I think, though, Joan, that we can go slower if we try."

Joan did not know what she could do about it; yet soon the tripod did slacken its pace, running at a speed considerably in excess of that of the early days, yet slow enough for us to catch the words.

"Listen," Stephen resumed. "You will agree with me that the earth is round, though you have never circled the globe; the proofs assigned appear to you to be reasonable. So it should be with the degrees of consciousness, the truth of which is indicated by modern science.

"Biology asserts that man is ascendant from a lower form of life; more and more the scientist hesitates to draw the line which shall definitely divide living matter and what you call inorganic matter. The physicists now hold light to be a form of electricity; in other words, they are coming to regard the phenomenon you know as electricity as evolutional and, therefore, as appearing in degrees. The original glimpse biological evolution afforded has become a more or less clear glimpse of cosmic evolution.

"And yet science has told but half the truth — the quantitative half. The thought that somewhere qualities must develop, just as do quantities in the so-called natural world, apparently has failed of recognition. What I propose is that science shall search out the nature of quality with as much industry as that displayed in its examination of quantity.

"That quantitative evolution on earth should have been accompanied by a quality development on another plane, real though unseen by man, is a thought wholly necessary to complete understanding of the actuality of evolution.

"Listen! Force, matter, chemical reaction, life, these constitute the ascent, qualitative as well as quantitative, of consciousness."

"And so," said Joan, when Stephen had finished, "it would appear, after all, that life sprang from matter?"

I wonder if I can make it quite clear that Stephen said no such thing. But let Stephen tell his own story.

"Force, matter, chemical reaction, life itself," he said, "are not, as you observe them, degrees of consciousness, strictly speaking. They are attributes of degrees of consciousness, manifestations of consciousness, if you will.

"My difficulty lies in a lack of earth terms, missing because earth does not see matter in its component parts. What I am about to say should, therefore, be accepted simply as suggestion, not as exact statement of fact.

"In the beginning, then, that never was consciousness was—an intangible existence, a whole of which quality and quantity were the halves. Now, consciousness by contact with itself intensified itself, just as two rays of light crossing each other might intensify the combined luminosity, just as your individual consciousness intensifies itself by contact with another individual's consciousness. And this intensification developed, let us say, the atom.

"For the atom to have been developed, it was, of course, essential that the atomic potentiality should have inhered in consciousness from the beginning.

"Science sets forth that the atom, in one form or another, is the basis of all matter, all energy.

The only thing I have to tell you is that it is the basis of all consciousness, of all degrees of consciousness from that intangible existence we have just postulated right up to supremacy itself. But keep clearly in mind that the atom is consciousness; nothing new was introduced; degree simply was developed.

"There was no creation; there is but the development of higher and higher degrees of consciousness. Yet for your understanding, think of consciousness as having created itself. This will not be so difficult a thought if you will recall how magnetic force creates itself through contact of two halves, the positive and the negative."

I looked up from setting down Stephen's words, and saw Joan's lips moving.

"What are you mumbling about?" I asked.

"I am saying my prayers," she answered; "at least I think I am, though I am not sure whether I have been listening to a sermon pointing the way to eternal bliss or to a lecture by a heretical professor bent on knocking the bottom out of Genesis."

"I have put a real bottom into Genesis," spelled Stephen, "by knocking a hypothetical one out. The story of a six-day creation is a great glimpse of the cosmic evolution. As for my 'sermons,' I wish there were a less dry way to tell you the things you must understand, but all good things come at a price. And the 'eternal bliss' part of it, Joan, is true. For just as surely as humanity regards life as its most precious possession, so it knows death as its only real fear. My gift to you is the elimination of fear. May I go on with the discussion?"

Joan consented.

"And now," Stephen continued, "our world is afloat, a world of force and matter, yet still consciousness. Finally, then, life makes its appearance, a degree higher than those that have gone before it, yet in its early form so low as scarcely to be called life at all. Behold what in earth terms is called protoplasm, a degree of consciousness infinitely primitive, but not so primitive as the original atom; protoplasm, let us say just for 'purposes of illumination, developed out of those degrees of consciousness manifested as force and matter, by way of an intervening degree known to you as chemical reaction. Behold the simple undifferentiated cell of living matter, capable of growth and reproduction."

"May I interrupt?" I asked.

"But surely," answered Stephen.

"Well," said I, "if soul is the quality of my consciousness, what is the quality of the consciousness of protoplasm?"

"Every degree of consciousness," spelled the tripod, "has its quality, its soul. Just as your consciousness is qualitative and quantitative, so also is protoplasmic consciousness."

"Do you mean," I asked, "that even protoplasm graduates into your plane?"

"But surely," answered Stephen. "All consciousness graduates out of the quantitative world of so-called nature into the qualitative world of supernature, and, too, the quality of protoplasm is reborn, just as truly as is the quality of human consciousness."

"But, Stephen," said Joan, "do you really mean that there is immortality even for life in its lowest? Do you see immortal protoplasm on your plane?"

"To both your questions, yes," Stephen answered. "Consciousness, many-degreed, is all there is, and of the all nothing can be lost. On this plane I see the degree of the quality of consciousness which corresponds to what you term protoplasm."

There was a pause. The tripod had been racing. After the pause it moved more slowly again.

"Listen!" Stephen continued. "Consciousness in kind is ever the same. Many are its degrees. Such general earth terms as force, matter, chemical reaction, and life give but slight conception of the variety of degree gradations. Observe the countless shades of life itself—the almost chemical activity of the weed, the but little less chemical life of the amoeba, the blind instinct of the bee, the reason-tinged instinct of the higher animals, finally the free-will degree of consciousness, man.

"Now, if force is force, whether it be gravitational or centrifugal, so life is life, whether it be the life of an amoeba or the life of a man. What is true of man's future development here on the qualitative plane must as well be true, in degree, of development of any form of life less than man.

"Man's consciousness is as it is only because through long eons of quantitative evolution on your plane, plus qualitative development on my plane, it has risen through birth and rebirth, step by step, degree by degree, from blind force to reason and free will. Evolution is an actuality more potent than earth theorists have dreamed.

"One thing more: All degrees of consciousness, human or less than human, are entities quite real. So real are degrees that an individual on my plane feels and sympathizes with the experience of his entire degree. This is also true of the individual on your plane, with the difference that, whereas we here understand, you there grope. Go ahead with your questions now. They will help."

"Perhaps," said Joan, "some of the moods that now and then so unaccountably take possession of us are really but the reflex of experiences other members of the same degree are undergoing."

"Exactly," Stephen replied. "Women are peculiarly sensitive in this respect. Many a woman in America has suffered intensely as the result of the experience, for example, of some war-stricken woman in France whom she of America has never heard of. Physicians in a future day will be on the lookout for the new diagnosis of certain hysterical disorders."

"What becomes of savages when they graduate?" I asked.

"They come to their degree here," answered Stephen. "They're off in their own reservation, as it were, though of course degrees here are no more physical than they are with you. The fact that persons of lower degrees on earth seek out their own kind is a glimpse. So, without knowing why, men in speaking of a seventh heaven have expressed a glimpse of the supreme degree and of the fact that it is attained by passage through lesser heavens or degrees."

"Well," I questioned, "can high degrees on your plane communicate with qualitative savages?"

"To be sure we can communicate with them," the ouija-board replied. "We aid them in their development."

"Do you have laws to control these savages?" I asked.

"Consciousness is the law," Stephen answered.

"Yes," said I, "but isn't consciousness the law here?"

"Surely," the ouija-board spelled, "but man does not allow it to rule."

"Can't the law be broken on the qualitative plane?" I asked.

"No," Stephen replied. "No more than you can break the law of gravitation."

"But," said I, "why doesn't the law of consciousness operate here as does the law of gravity?"

"Man's free will," Stephen answered.

"Your will, too, is free," I argued.

"Yes," Stephen responded, "but we see here not as through a glass darkly."

Joan spoke. "Why fuss over savages?" she said. "Stephen, the world has broached many definitions of genius. Men of genius have been called everything from gods to maniacs."

"There are two kinds of geniuses," answered Stephen's tripod. "There is the man who is, as you say, psychic. His work is wonderful; yet, when men meet him face to face, they find his personality unsatisfactory. Such a man simply puts into words the thoughts of some greater mentality living here. The world calls this type of man a genius, yet—I speak without disparagement of his gift—he is not truly so.

"The true man of genius is one whose degree of consciousness is unusually high. His quality was vouchsafed him from a degree here approaching the supreme. The recognition the world gives him will depend in large measure on how completely he fulfils that degree of quality by development of proportionate quantity. Of course, high quality, too, may be, and in fact often is, psychic."

"Well," said I, "if genius of exalted order can exist on earth, and if, at the same time, savages return on graduation to that degree of consciousness which on your plane corresponds to their degree here, it follows that earth has many individuals of a consciousness higher than the lower degrees of your plane."

"But surely," answered Stephen. "Remember, however, that in the end all consciousness must reach supreme."

"Stephen," I sam, "we have but to place our hands upon this tripod and you come. Are you always within call?"

"Always to your degree," he answered. "For your degree and Joan's is my own. We are three of practically the same degree. That is why I am able so easily to communicate with you."

XXIV

THE AFTER-LIFE

"FOLLOWING Stephen's discussion of degrees, Joan and I stumbled into our typewriter experiment. Though at first the typewriter promised to expedite matters, it quickly became apparent that the pressure of my hands on Joan's temples distressed her. Thereupon it seemed that Stephen did not wish to risk discussion of the next subject, which was to be, he said, rebirth of consciousness. And even when we returned to the ouija-board, Stephen, for some reason or other, continued to talk generally. Perhaps he was awaiting Joan's suggestion that resulted in direct mental communication. Then, with the mental method finally hit upon, the fact that at first I was required to hold Joan's wrists made my continuance of the record impossible; the philosophy was not formally resumed until my hands were freed.

This period of delay, however, offered a number of interesting, though digressive, conversations. The talks that follow represent a part of the communications received on the typewriter and during the final days of the ouija-board.

"If I should die to-night what would be my first thought on entering the after-life?" I asked.

"Well, in the first place, you would simply come to," Stephen answered. "Your coming to would be just as natural as awakening from sleep. And doubtless your first thought would be, 'It is all true, just as Stephen told me.'"

I asked what I would see first.

"Your nurse, of course," Stephen retorted. "Haven't I told you that some one of us will be on hand to hold your head and persuade you that really the operation is over, and that, after all, it didn't kill you!"

"And what will the nurse look like?" I asked.

"Well," said Stephen, "all consciousness has form. When you come here and your eyes are unsealed, those who meet you will seem quite natural and quite human, as, indeed, we are. In fact, we are more human than you, as you now know yourself, ever dreamed of being. We are humanity intensified many times. Would it be interesting if I were to repeat to you some of the exclamations of one who came to us to-day—a sensitive woman who here is finding plainly visible all that on earth she but vaguely divined?"

"Very interesting," I said.

Whereupon Stephen continued:

"When this woman met and recognized a friend who had graduated some years ago, she said: 'Why, Winifred dear, what a very lovely face!—in form, just such a face as one might see on the earth-plane, but that is all. The coloring is so marvelous. Such wonderful eyes! They are like light. The face shines like a piece of exquisite white Tiffany glass, tinted in the delicate, yet intense pastel shades. It seems as if there were a number of electric lights inside and beaming through. Your face, Winifred, is glorified, ethereal. It is like a thin cloud over the sun. Your body is draped in colors. All the many other persons whom I see are draped in colors, but each is dressed differently. According to their wishes, you say? Oh yes, according to their thoughts—I understand. It is their thoughts that clothe them. It is a beautiful world here. It isn't crowded, though there are all sorts of things—trees and flowers. At first I didn't recognize the trees; they seemed so alive-like, so happy. And through all these things I can see. These beautiful forms— yours, and those of the trees and the flowers, of the birds—are the materiality of the qualitative plane? The whole thing seems to resolve itself down to the intensity of the perceptions. One way you look at the experience earth knows as death, it is simply the releasing of the senses.'"

Stephen spoke then in his own character, saying:

"The woman was right. Of a fact, death is the freeing of the senses. It releases a man from the encumbering shell of his body. It is, therefore, not the end, but rather the beginning. Earth life is a training-school for graduation and the freedom that graduation brings. And not only is death a releasing of the senses; it is a freeing of the subconscious mind."

Stephen's last statement may mean much or little, but for me the words "freedom of the subconscious" contain a wonderful thought. I said so.

"I doubt," said Stephen, "if you appreciate how wonderful. It is this way: All you have seen and heard and felt and thought out is as truly in your mind as the thought of which you are at this instant conscious. The psychologist will tell you this is true. Your conscious mind may fail to remember, but your subconscious mind forgets nothing. Think of the marvel of releasing that subconscious mind, of being in instant possession of all of your experience rather than just that trifle which at any given moment you are able by the association of ideas to summon up. All broader theories of education rest on the glimpsed truth of my plane's freedom of the subconscious. In this fact find the reason for the faith that prompts men arduously to master the thousand and one studies they forthwith forget.

"When individual consciousnesses come here, their first sensation that is unusual is their freedom—freedom of perception, of thought, of movement. Graduation is the intensification of earthly consciousness and the granting of freedom to it.

"Do not misunderstand. The same degree of freedom is not acquired by all who come. Life here for all is equally free in the sense that each attains opportunity for qualitative development. But even so there are differences in the degrees of development severally achieved. In one degree we have less of understanding and, therefore, in one sense of the word, less of freedom; in a higher degree we win more."

"Are you everywhere at once?" Joan asked.

"Did I say so?" answered Stephen. "You call, and it is as though I were in a distant city. I get your telegram—the method of transmission is just as material; and I come, without boarding a train."

"And you come in your bodily presence?"

"But surely," Stephen replied. "At this instant I am standing with my hand on your shoulder."

Such a remark a few weeks before would have caused Joan to shrink away. But one gets used to unseen hands, especially when they are unfelt as well. She asked, "How did you get into the room?"

Stephen answered with a question of his own: "Do you know how light penetrates matter? Do you understand transparency?"

"Does one have a home on the qualitative plane?" I asked.

"We have our degrees," answered Stephen, "and our circles within our degrees. A thought, if entertained by two or more, may be to them a home."

"What of families?" Joan asked. "Does one recognize his father as his father?"

"But surely," Stephen replied. "We on the qualitative plane know our earth kin as such. But here again remember that consciousness is a whole. In a final analysis the special relations of parts must be interpreted in the light of their general relation. The family tie is a tie of natural evolution, and it is, of course, worthy. It does not follow, however, that the family tie is a spiritual tie, though members of a given family may be of the same degree and, therefore, united with one another in a sympathy that transcends their mere blood relationship. On the other hand, brother even on earth may not find his closest friend in brother."

"What of sex?" I asked.

"In heaven," said Stephen, "there is neither marriage nor giving in marriage. There is no sex here as you know it. There is in consciousness what an electrician might be tempted to call a negative and positive division. And that division, manifesting itself on earth as sex, runs through the whole of consciousness. Here there is a parallel to what you know as sex, and I am told the parallel reaches even into supremacy. But there is no birth here; birth is a natural phenomenon, serving the development of quantity."

"I suppose," ventured Joan, "rebirth brings the quality of the consciousness of men back to earth as women and that of women back as men."

"I suppose no such thing," answered Stephen. "Would you have the consciousness of Darby other than it is?"

"But," I offered, "how broadening it would be if the individual consciousness might, through rebirth, win both the man's experience and the woman's!"

"If a man truly loves a woman," Stephen replied, "he will develop through her, because of his sympathy for her. The converse also."

'Does a person just graduated attend his own funeral?" I asked.

"Surely I have already indicated to you," answered Stephen, "that we do not let newcomers do that. We take them away from it all. They are still pretty human, pretty close still to the earth consciousness. Sometimes, though, when there is great love, we do let them go back, and, all unsuspected, they comfort those who are left behind. More often the comforter is not the one just gone, but some one else."

"There must be many odd meetings," I said. "For instance, that of the murdered man and his slayer."

"These two need not meet," was the response. "Yet if they choose to, it will be with fuller understanding than either possessed in earth life. There is no evil, only negatives. And here on the qualitative plane there are no negatives in the sense that lack of development in one individual can work harm to another. Forgiveness for injuries done one on earth is easy here where consciousness in development is adequately comprehended."

"Stephen," said Joan, "don't you ever tire? Don't you ever sleep?"

"Why should I tire?" he answered. "Why should I sleep? There is no tiring here on the qualitative plane. The soul, quality, never tires. This is true even on your plane. Only your body grows weary."

"But," Joan continued, "you, too, on your own confession, have a material body. Why should my body tire, while yours does not?"

"Occasionally," said Stephen, "the world talks of aurae, sometimes of astral bodies. Whether it will be possible for me to separate the glimpse from the emotional hypotheses involved is doubtful, but I shall try.

"In the first place, I have told you that I have form and that that form is material. It is not, however, correct to compare my form with what you call your body. After all, your natural body only reflects the true form of your consciousness.

"You must, of course, take into account the fact that your body has of itself consciousness quite distinct from your own. In a sense, your body may be said to be a stress point of various cellular forces. It is, as the physiologist puts it, composed of a vast number of cells, independent of one another, yet so related as to constitute a whole. Now, each of these cells has a life of its own, a consciousness of its own. A man's arm may be cut off without in the least affecting his self-awareness.

"The fact is that your consciousness on the earth-plane is associated always with degrees of consciousness lower than itself. The lower degrees, the cells of your body, constitute the house in which you live. The form of your own consciousness should not be confused with the form of the bodily cells with which on earth you are associated. Nevertheless, the true form of a man's consciousness is the cast that molds the features of his body."

"Then," said I, "a person physically beautiful must also be beautiful of soul?"

"Not necessarily," answered Stephen. "A very beautiful flower need have no scent. Your inference is the result of your failing to take account of what I told you about the natural body having of itself consciousness."

Joan and I believe that Stephen's thought of a form attribute quite distinct from the natural body is important to his philosophy. Yet the matter is not easy of comprehension. Such a thought does, however, relieve Stephen's philosophy from the necessity of assuming that the soul liberated by death must somehow, somewhere acquire a new body. The truth seems to be that such a soul merely comes into knowledge of its real body, which in earth life is not —whatever it may be—the flesh-and-blood affair of cells that, while they serve man's consciousness, pursue, nonetheless, their own ends.

"We here," Stephen added, "are not subject to fatigue, because we are unassociated with lower materiality than our own. Fatigue is threatened disintegration of the cells of your natural body. Your every thought and every act tend to break down those cells. Through disease they are actually disintegrated. Here I am dissociated from that combination of lesser degrees of consciousness which on earth I called my body. Here there is neither fatigue nor disease."

XXV

THE REBIRTH OF CONSCIOUSNESS

I THINK Stephen's rebirth idea proved hardest of all for me to understand. It seemed at first wholly bizarre. And then, too, I was not yet fully adjusted to the phenomenon of mental communication.

For weeks I had been accustomed to address a question into the air and have it answered on the ouija-board; the performance had ceased to be bewildering. But to say, "Stephen, what about this?" or, "How about that, Stephen?" and have Joan herself answer, was a different matter, especially as Joan's own personality seemed, as I touched her wrist, to fade away, giving place to that of an unseen some one else.

It may be that the atmosphere of the rebirth discussion and of the conversations that followed it would be more faithfully reported if I dropped the old phrases, "Stephen said" and "Stephen answered," and adopted instead "Joan said, speaking for Stephen." I do not do so for the reason that before many evenings had passed what might be called the Joan Stephen became as much a matter of course as the ouija-board Stephen had been. Indeed, had I been able by closing my eyes to have forgotten Joan's presence, I might well have fancied, even during the rebirth discussion, that

Stephen himself was sitting beside me. But just at first such forgetfulness was not possible; Joan's assumption of personality not her own was still too novel.

"Rebirth is not in any sense what you know as reincarnation," Stephen began. "It is true, as I once told you, that in the reincarnation idea there lies a glimpse. But this Buddhistic thought is on the whole an emotional hypothesis. Dismiss once and for all any possibility of my meaning by rebirth what the world has meant by reincarnation."

"Very well, Stephen," I said, "the thought is dismissed. I never lived individually prior to my present existence, and never after my death shall I live here on earth again. That is what you would have me first understand, is it not?"

"Absolutely," he answered.

"But," cried I, "what is there about mortal other than himself to be reborn?"

"A part of his consciousness is reborn, not once, but many times," Stephen replied.

"What part?" I demanded.

"I have already told you that the quality of consciousness is reborn."

"Is, then, a man's consciousness divisible?"

"But, Darby," Stephen replied, "cannot a thing give of its quality without being itself divided?"

"Absurd!" I said. "How can my individual consciousness go forward after death and at the same time the quality of my consciousness return to this world?"

Before my words were finished Stephen was answering.

"Listen!" he said. "Let us in imagination visit a phonograph company's laboratory. Everything is in readiness for the making of a record. The singer lifts her voice. In the days that follow records of the song find their way into thousands of homes, where at the push of a lever the soprano's voice is heard over and over again. Now does it follow that, because the quality of that soprano's voice has lent itself to the phonographic record, the soprano herself, or her voice, has ceased to exist? Absurd!"

But Stephen's thought was beyond me.

"Do you understand, Joan?" I asked.

"This is Stephen talking," came the reply. "Suppose you touch Joan's wrist, then read her your notes."

Stephen vanished, Joan at my touch returning. She listened attentively to the words she had just spoken, quite as though she had never heard them before.

"I cannot understand this rebirth notion," I said.

"Why," said she, "it's not so obscure. You express your thoughts, yet you continue. What happens in the case of the phonograph happens in another way every time you give me an idea. I don't know that I actually understand what Stephen calls the rebirth of quality, but I can conceive its possibility. The phonograph illustration simply applies the law of parallels."

I was dogged. It seemed to me, I said, that in the present case the only parallel amounting to anything more than a mere analogy must lie between natural birth and whatever it was Stephen called rebirth.

"Well, you and Stephen fight it out," said Joan. "Frankly, I'm glad I don't have to listen to the argument."

I touched her wrist again—silence a moment, then Stephen.

"Just so," he said. "Birth and rebirth are parallels. Take an oak-tree. In season it puts forth its acorn. And the acorn ripens and falls to earth. It is a bit of what you call matter. Chemical analysis can determine just what elements and just what combinations of those elements go to make up that material acorn. This quantitative analysis presents no difficulty whatever to the earth scientist.

"Yet imagine that acorn picked up by a chemist who had never seen a seed before. Such a chemist, for all his quantitative analysis, would scarcely recognize the acorn as anything differing greatly from a chip of wood. If, however, he dropped that acorn in a fitting soil, there would spring from it another oak tree. Then he would become aware of the acorn's essential quality, of its potential treeness.

"How, now, did the acorn come by its quality of treeness?"

"Why," I said, "from the parent tree, of course."

"Granted your answer were wholly correct," replied Stephen, "would it follow that the parent tree is any less an individual tree because it gave to the acorn its own quality?"

"Well, no," I admitted, "I suppose not."

"Neither," said Stephen, "is the individual on my plane, whose quality of consciousness is born back into your plane, thereby rendered any less an individual.

"In bodily form are not you a man and Joan a woman? Were your parents any the less corporeal men and women for having endowed you, in the process of natural birth, with human form? Now, in a fashion quite parallel to that birth-endowment of body, rebirth from my plane gave you your qualitative endowment. Birth and rebirth operate under parallel laws."

"But, Stephen," I said, "why is it not reasonable to suppose that the parent endows its offspring not only with bodily form, but quality of consciousness as well? Why must a qualitative rebirth be conjured up to explain what simple natural birth might as easily account for?"

"Listen!" Stephen answered. "Go back to the making of the phonograph record. If natural birth were all, if there were no rebirth of consciousness out of my qualitatively free plane into yours, which is qualitatively determined, there would be no evolution. The phonographic record is but a replica.

"Natural birth implies reproduction only, the endless passing on from parents to offspring of identically that which the parents received from their parents. It is rebirth from out the qualitatively free plane into the qualitatively fixed plane that makes of simple reproduction the actuality of evolution. I have given you this thought before; it is a distinct contribution to scientific truth.

"Certain it is that the only creation which ever was or ever will be is the evolution of consciousness out of lower degrees into higher. Yet development on your plane is quantitative only. Whence, then, the qualitative advance that your evolutionist has noted? Do you not see, Darby, the necessity of a qualitatively free mode of being? Such a plane must be postulated by the evolutionist himself. He will be forced into the hypothesis just as soon as he recognizes the qualitatively fixed character of all consciousness of the so-called natural world. Except for rebirth out of the plane of qualitative development could there be any evolution? What I tell you is reasonable."

"It would seem so, Stephen," I said. "But, tell me, whose quality of consciousness lives again in me?"

"The quality of certain artists and philosophers," Stephen answered.

And with that we were again plunged into misunderstanding; for I had gathered that, though the quality of the individual and not the individual himself is reborn, each person here represents the quality of some certain other person there. When Stephen stated that the quality of many had been reborn into me, I found myself again groping.

"Listen, now!" he said, when I told him my difficulty. "Rebirth is the coming back into your world of a higher quality of consciousness which has before been in your world in a lower degree. Now this does not mean individual quality of consciousness.

"To illustrate: The housewife has a tub of water. She dips out a pailful. That pail of water, let us say, stands to the tub of water as the individual consciousness of a living man stands to the degree of consciousness from which at birth he was qualitatively endowed.

"Now the housewife puts a few drops of bluing into the pail and then turns its contents back into the tub. Whereupon it distributes its blueness throughout the water's whole.

"Next the housewife dips out another pailful. Is it not apparent that the second pailful may contain much, little, or possibly none of the water of the first pailful? So it is with rebirth."

"You make your point, Stephen," I said. "Degree quality, not individual quality, is reborn. But why complicate your illustration by introducing the bluing angle? The thing would have been quite as clear had you kept to just plain water."

"Because," answered Stephen, "I wanted to kill two birds with one stone. The bluing the housewife dropped into the first pail colors the whole of the tub. But the housewife wishes the entire tubful of water to be as blue as the pailful. Therefore, to her second pailful she adds more bluing, turning it, too, back into the tub, and thereby further intensifying the tubful's blue. And now she repeats this process over and over again until the desired shade is acquired by the tub's whole.

"In like fashion consciousness is qualitatively reborn into your world for the purpose of quantitative development; and each individual, bearing back his gift of quantity to the whole, leavens the whole, gives it greater potentiality for the development of quality with which to be reborn for the purpose of further quantitative development."

"Is reason reborn?" I asked.

"You know better," Stephen answered. "It is the quality of consciousness, not the attributes of consciousness, that is reborn. The potentiality of the attributes is, of course, present at birth, but they must be developed by each individual for himself. Each individual must himself develop his reason, his will, his memory, his perceptions. Otherwise, you can understand, rebirth would be of quantity as well as of quality."

After a minute or two of silence Stephen said: "Touch Joan's wrist. She is tired." Again he vanished.

"Is the argument over?" Joan asked. But, upon my reading her Stephen's words, she herself did a little groping.

"Stephen once indicated," she said, "that people sometimes have glimpses of the previous existence of their quality. He said that the first time he visited England certain places seemed familiar to him. How could that be if the attribute of memory is not reborn? Ask him, Darby."

When communication was resumed Stephen answered: "Take three graduated men. One was a success in business, one in a profession, one in art, all to the same degree in their various lines. In other words, upon graduation they brought the same quantity here. But, inasmuch as their callings were different, their associations different, you know that wholly different experiences developed that quantity in those men; and naturally their quantities were colored by the attributes that served them. Now, while the attributes of these men are never reborn, yet the impress of those attributes is left on the quantity which their use developed and on the resulting quality. When, then, these men's degree of quality is given as an endowment to a child, that quality is colored by those former developing influences. There are things you speak of as knowing intuitively. Tell Joan—but do not disturb her now; the connection is good—that intuition so called is but the state or color of the individual's degree of quality."

"So then," I said, "what I do now is a concern not only of my own future development, but of the development of my entire degree as it is reborn into the world years after I have left the world."

"Unto the third and fourth generation," quoted Stephen, "and to their children's children.

"It is to be expected," he added, "that men will better understand the laws of heredity when they understand the truth of rebirth."

"Even as you spoke," I said, "I was thinking that the inevitableness of quality's rebirth reduces control of heredity to a rather sorry state. You say there are low degrees where you are. If I understand you rightly, these low degrees will be, in fact must be, reborn into this world."

"Surely," Stephen replied. "It is unconscious recognition of this truth that causes the world to show its wisdom in such reforms as birth control. A man and woman of inferior quality can give birth to an even lower degree than their own. Criminals can and are likely to produce greater criminals than themselves."

"That's the point," I urged. "What's the use in attempting to restrict such mating if low quality must be born back into the world?"

"Any form of birth control," answered Stephen, "that has as its object the restriction of the offspring of persons of very low degree shows the world's increasing wisdom. Two persons, both low, call to earth in the process of natural reproduction low quality, just as persons of high degree call high quality. That is true, and it is also true that quality must be reborn.

"But, listen! I have shown how the individual's gift of quantity leavens the whole of his degree. And have I not made it clear that there is at the same time a leavening of the great whole? Quality must be reborn, but can you not see that the leavening of the whole must ultimately raise the quality of the lower degrees here? Until that leavening is accomplished, low quality is served best by my world."

"Stephen," I said, "you have asserted that even protoplasm graduates to your plane and that forth from your plane its quality of consciousness is born back into this world of mine. Well, it follows, then, that all animals, all plants, die in my world to live in yours, and qualitatively to be reborn. Is this true?"

211

"But surely," Stephen replied. "And your only difficulty in grasping this thought will lie in the preconceived ideas you have of this world of mine. Naturally you can conceive of no form other than forms you have seen. I have a body, to be sure; and your body is a glimpse of mine. But my body is, to use St. Paul's word, a glorified body, a form beyond the reach of your ordinary perceptions, beyond your imagination.

"Now when plant or animal life graduates into the qualitative plane its form is not any bodily form you are familiar with. Yet the consciousness of the plant or animal you call dead is just as surely here, and as individually so, as I am. More than one man who has loved a dog has insisted on a dog heaven, and in that insistence he expressed a glimpse of the truth.

"There is no offense to the human mind in asking it to conceive of human beings surviving death in a form resembling their earthly bodies; but man's egotism is shocked when he is asked to believe that creatures in forms resembling animals are, so to speak, the associates of the angels. But if you will admit your ignorance of all qualitative forms, the difficulty will not seem so great."

XXVI

QUALITATIVE DEVELOPMENT

WHAT an oddity it was that in grasping each new particular of Stephen's scheme I found it necessary to grasp much of its whole over again! Pluralistic monism had succeeded in setting me straight as to man's individualistic survival. And I could imagine the individual supremacy of man. But it was hard to conceive, for instance, that even a tree survives death. It seemed improbable that the tree should survive as an individual and impossible that as an individual it should go on developing. I could not imagine a supreme tree.

"How long, how long!" wailed Stephen. "If you could but forget preconceived ideas! If you would but study the reasonableness of that which I tell you!

"Let us start all over again. Your first difficulty is that you doubt the individuality of the earth tree. You think it a mere composite of branches and twigs and leaves. It is true the tree puts forth leaves and blossoms. But do you not grow hair and finger nails? These are not of the essence of the consciousness which is you, nor are the tree's leaves of the essence of the consciousness which is the tree. The life of the tree is not a composite; it is an entity, just as your life is an entity. The tree which you see is a manifestation of a producing force called by you plant life, just as you are a manifestation of animal life. You recognize the individualistic character of all animal life; I think you must also admit the individualistic character of all plant life. Tree life manifests itself now as a hickory and now as a palm. And no two hickory-trees or palm-trees are just alike; such is the distinctiveness of their individuality.

"Now let us trace the development, from earth manifestation on, of an individual tree—for example, an oak-tree. The oak-tree matures and is hewn down. As a material entity it remains in the form of whatever man fashions it into. The life of it has vanished from your sight, and you have just as much right to ask what becomes of the life of that tree as you have to ponder what becomes of the individual person's life when he is hewn down by death. Where has the life of that oak-tree gone? It has gone back, as an individual tree, to its qualitative degree.

"Now the degree of quality to which the oak tree returns—which is made up of many individual tree qualities—is subject to the same development that every other degree of consciousness is subject to. The tree, therefore, gives of itself in rebirth. It is leavened by quantity. It goes on developing individually. It continues on to the supreme degree, stamped always by its individual experience plus its assimilation through leavening.

"I have told you the form attribute of consciousness is manifested in the supreme. What the various form attributes there are I have not told you and cannot tell you; there are no earth terms by which supreme form can be made clear to you. I do tell you this: The form attributes of the supreme are not necessarily all alike; all supremacy is individualistic, and consequently characteristic. That is as much as I can say."

"But," I asked, "does the tree as it develops ever become comparable to a man?"

"Yes," answered Stephen, "but it is the comparison I cannot explain to you."

"Can it be," I asked, "that in what I might call the human degree there are on your side individuals who never lived on earth as men?"

"But surely," answered Stephen.

"Such individuals," I suggested, "cannot be the equals of what might be termed their more strictly human fellows."

"Surely they can be and are," Stephen answered. "Else how could they be of the given degree?"

"It is a difficult thought, Stephen," I said. "Granted the plane of qualitative development, how is it possible for that life which manifests itself here as a tree ever to develop a quality that will make it the equal of man? What's the process of that development?"

Said Stephen: "Naturally enough you, who are familiar only with quantitative development, cannot imagine the process of qualitative development, and you lack terms by which I might describe it to you. I can only point out to you that such development is reasonably indicated by your own knowledge. Perhaps an illustration would help clear the difficulty."

There was silence for a space. Then Stephen said: "Consider the quantitative development of a stone on your plane. Take, for example, a piece of sandstone. As such it cannot serve as food for plant life. A seed dropped on the piece of sandstone would never germinate. Now, after a long time infinitesimal and invisible motion wears this piece of sandstone down to its component grains of sand; the sandstone becomes a part of the soil. It becomes fertile and develops a definite service to plant life. It aids in germination. It has a new function. It has developed quantity. And yet it is still just sand. It is changed in form; it is changed as quantity, but that is all. With this simple bit of natural and empirical knowledge in mind, is it then impossible for you to conceive that the stone might, somewhere and under some circumstances, qualitatively progress?"

It is a convincing trait of this thing we call Stephen that it can be turned aside by no argument of mine or Joan's. From the beginning we noticed this characteristic, and it was one of the things that prevented our ready acceptance of Stephen and his philosophy as the subconscious products of our own minds. Having taken a position, Stephen would maintain it with a resource of argument that was the constant object of our wonderment. I might not be able to imagine the survival and qualitative development of a tree; endlessly, it seemed, Stephen could cite facts "reasonably indicating" that tree's eternal progress.

"It is interesting," I said, "to speculate on the possibility of my consciousness having been once of the tree degree."

"How," spelled Stephen, "do you explain the great love and understanding some men have for the beauties and moods of nature? It is because their quality of consciousness happens to have much of the more potentially exquisite forms of nature in it. The artist portraying a sunset, a sea, a landscape, may have once been of their consciousness. He puts that part of his soul on canvas. But note that, though the quality which once was the quality of treeness may be in one man and give to him a deep understanding of the woods, it may in another man be lacking."

"It would seem, however, reasonable to suppose it present in all men," I ventured.

"I expected you to say as much," answered Stephen. "Thus soon you have forgotten the housewife's bluing. Well, take a pint of water and pour into it a measure of oil. Now shake the two, thoroughly mixing them. You will agree that as an entirety the water and oil are pretty well mixed. Now draw out a drop. That drop may have much oil in it, little or none. So it is with degrees, as they are leavened by the individual gifts of quantity, and as their quality is reborn."

"You say all consciousness is reborn, Stephen?" I asked.

"All consciousness is reborn qualitatively," he answered, "except that of supremacy."

XXVII

MATERIAL THINGS

A DOUBT had entered my mind. Had the intricacies of the philosophy invited coloring? I would ask Stephen. But might not the question be futile? How could I be sure the answer itself would be uninfluenced by Joan's personal opinion?

The evening Stephen announced matter as the subject of discussion I said to him, "If you really do see, as you say you do, read the words I am about to write out, and answer the question they ask."

I wrote this question, "Has the philosophy you have given Joan and me been colored?"

"Stephen," I said, "can you read the words I have written?"

"But surely," he replied. "But I cannot answer your question at this time. The receiving station realizes that a test is being imposed. I'll try to get the answer through in the midst of other matter."

I was skeptical of the outcome. At last, I thought, I had cornered this Stephen who sees, but is himself unseen. And yet before the evening was over he had answered my question.

He was saying, "Men imagine that materiality is a fundamental." He hesitated a moment, I remember. Then he continued: "Could they see matter as it really is, they would understand that the thing they have been calling matter is in reality an attribute of a fundamental.—There is no coloring to speak of.—That fundamental is consciousness, consciousness in degrees."

Beyond doubt my question had been answered. Was there really a Stephen and had he really seen my written words, unseen surely by the blindfolded Joan?

The happening suggested another experiment. If it was possible for Stephen to read words unseen by Joan, would it not also be possible for Joan, acting under his direction, to imitate any gesture I might make, such as the opening and closing of my hand?

"Let's try," said Stephen. "I am in good control of the station to-night. Because she has no interest whatever in the subject of matter, her conscious mind is more dormant than usual."

To make doubly sure that Joan could see nothing, I reinforced the blindfold she customarily wore with a second handkerchief, Then, in silence, I raised my hand to my forehead. Joan hesitated a moment, brought her hand half-way up, paused, then executed a most military salute. Next I raised my arm and held my hand on the level of my shoulder. Joan held her hand out, but raised it only halfway to shoulder level. I then leaned over as though to pick something up from the floor. Joan seemed confused, but after a while she, too, leaned over in her chair and reached toward the floor. I raised both hands over my head. Joan made a motion as though to imitate me, but before her hands reached far she dropped them listlessly in her lap. I tried other gestures, but none of them was imitated.

Finally Stephen spoke. "That is enough," he said. "The experiment succeeded better than I thought it would. Now let us go on with the discussion."

And so we resumed our talk on the nature of matter, the discussion extending over several evenings. From time to time I would touch Joan's wrist, thus signaling a break in the communication, and would read her Stephen's words. "Pointless theories!" she would exclaim. Stephen, on re-establishment of communication, would ask me to assure Joan for him that in the end she would recognize practical worth in his theories. Once the professor appeared and said: "Let Joan have patience. For the proper exposition of a thought of any complexity it is essential that an adequate foundation be laid."

Even so, Joan's impatience was, I am sure, justified. My failure readily to understand the corollaries of Stephen's saying, "Matter is the form attribute of consciousness," resulted in many repetitions both in the questions I asked and in Stephen's answers. I offer here but a summary of the discussion.

Asserting matter to be the form attribute of consciousness, Stephen stated that form is characteristic of all consciousness—of that consciousness which is the stone, of human consciousness, of graduated consciousness. Human consciousness has a form, or materiality, invisible to the human eye; this is, of course, distinct from the physical body. Stephen's consciousness likewise possesses a material form, and this, too, is ordinarily invisible to the eye of man.

"Now," said Stephen, "you can see the form of the lower degree of consciousness which you call matter. Because the form of the stone is all you do see you mistake that form, that attribute, for reality itself. In truth, though, the reality of the stone is none other in kind than your own self of self. It is consciousness, an infinitely low degree."

Again he said:

"I have already referred to the fact that many physicists regard light as a form of electrical energy. That is to say, light and electricity are held to be one and the same thing, differing not in kind, but in degree. And yet to your every-day senses, and those even of the scientists, light and electricity remain, as before, two entirely distinct entities.

"If, then, you are willing in the one case, that of electricity and light, to throw aside the testimony of your senses, and accept instead the experimentally deduced conclusions of science, must you struggle over-much in accepting the likeness in kind of all energy? If light and electricity are degree manifestations of one fundamental, may it not be that gravitation and the many other apparently distinct energies are further degrees thereof? Now, could you see matter in what, for your understanding, I have called its component parts, you would the more readily grasp the thought of a fundamental inclusive, not only of force, but of matter itself."

Later he said: "Occasionally science glimpses matter as a complex of stress knots—one might say, force ganglia. That is a very wonderful glimpse. Yet, with the force theory of matter demonstrated, science would scarcely have solved any metaphysical problem. Surely we could substitute the word 'force' for 'matter' throughout this discussion, and our argument would lose none of its controversy, as, indeed, we could substitute the word 'reason' or the word 'will.' Force is an attribute of consciousness just as truly as is matter or will."

"And yet," I said, "reducing matter to terms of force does help to elucidate your contention that the fundamental of human consciousness and the fundamental of matter are alike in kind. Consciousness as spirituality is force after a fashion; it is at least analogous to force in a way matter doesn't seem to be. But if matter can be scientifically defined as an appearance set up by combinations of forces unseen as such by men, then it is much easier to understand the likeness in kind of matter and life."

"It is fine to hear you say so," Stephen said. "I can appreciate the difficulty you encounter when you attempt to apply the word 'consciousness' to inanimate matter. But you realize that I do not mean to say that inanimate matter possesses self-awareness. I say only that that degree of the one reality which manifests itself to you materially is possessed of the potentiality of self-awareness."

He added: "Many attempts have been made to explain the one reality in terms of matter and force. But why define reality in its lowest terms? I choose to define it in terms of its highest earth development, man's self of self, Because man's knowledge of the external world is empirical, matter can scarcely be made the standard of reality. The one reality above all dispute is the individual man's feel of himself. In it alone can a satisfactory standard of reality be found."

"I presume," I said, "that the consciousness manifest to me as matter develops?"

"I have so indicated," Stephen answered. "But there are no terms in which I can explain to you matter's graduation or rebirth."

"But," I argued, "in the course of that development is not the law of matter's indestructibility broken down? The thing I know as matter will have vanished."

"Not at all," answered Stephen. "In such a case the low degree will simply have developed into a higher. Your theory of the indestructibility of matter is a quantitative formula. Now what I tell you is that all consciousness survives not only quantitative changes, but qualitative also. I ask you to recognize the indestructibility, quantitative and qualitative, of all consciousness, whether that of a stone or a man. And, using the word 'matter' again in its accurate sense, as the attribute of a given degree of consciousness rather than as consciousness itself, I say to you that even as an attribute matter is eternal—all consciousness, even the supreme, has form."

XXVIII

SUPREMACY AND GOD

ONE of the most interesting of Stephen's discussions was on the character of God and that ultimate goal which he so hopefully insists all must reach, and which he has termed "Supremacy."

As I go over my notes I find that I asked a number of questions scarcely relevant to the subject, yet interesting in view of the answers they called forth. The questions and answers follow.

Q.—Where do babies go when they die?

A.—Back to the degree from which they were born.

Q.—Those that die too young to have developed any quantity at all? A.—But surely.

Q.—Have they an opportunity for development there?

A.—Indeed yes. Lacking great quantitative development of their own, they share, through leavening, in the quantitative gift each individual of their degree brings from earth.

Q.—You said sudden death was the one great tragedy. Is this true also for little children? (This question was prompted by the accidental death of a child living in our neighborhood.)

A.—Children are so close to that from which they came that a sudden going back is for them no tragedy. Earth has not had time to submerge completely their knowledge of our great everywhere. Sudden graduation is startling only for those who have been so educated that they no longer remember their eternal youth, and even they are soon met and cared for, as I have told you.

Q.—Is the idea of purgatory a glimpse?

A.—But surely. There are many mansions in the house of consciousness. One of those mansions is life as you know it; another is life as I know it; and many are the mansions that line the road both you and I must travel before we reach supremacy.

Q.—How do you recognize one another on the qualitative plane?

A.—We recognize one another not facially, as men recognize each other, but by the individual degree of quality.

Q.—Why don't we here on earth recognize one another in the same way?

A.—You do; only you fail to note the fact. Often you recognize what you call soul in an individual the very first time you meet that person. Take, for example, the so-called instinctive likes of animals, of infantile minds and blind persons.

Q.—Will man on earth ever evolve into a higher species?

A.—That is a difficult question. As an affair of nature, biological evolution is largely the result of adaptation on the part of the living organism to its environment. Man is already so high in the scale that to a great extent he is master of his environment—that is, he adapts his environment to himself. However, there are great changes of perception and mentality in store for man. For example, let your senses broaden their present scope, and the veil between my plane and yours will be lifted.

Q.—There would, in truth, be no death then, would there?

A.—There is no death now. There is only failure to recognize graduation as such.

Q.—What will happen when the physical conditions of earth no longer can support life?

A.—Earth has already developed many new earths out of the old earths that have passed away. Your man of scientific research tells you this, and you believe. He also knows there are, must be, new earths to come. I tell you there will be new heavens, too.

The supremacy discussion, in which the foregoing questions and answers were embedded, began with Stephen's saying: "Three things I have told you about the supreme degree of consciousness. First, in the beginning, which never was, every particle of the all possessed the potentiality of supremacy, so that all that is must ultimately become supreme. Second, there are those who have reached supremacy. Third, from out the supreme degree there is no rebirth.

"Now the supreme degree is made up of individual consciousnesses. It is the quintessence of pluralistic monism. As a whole it is a thing of absolute oneness. For the individual it is the height of self-realization.

"Experience, we have seen, indicates that all things are, in any analysis approaching finality, individualistic. The scientist speaks of the atom, the electron. Your own observation teaches you individuality pervades life. Every such individual particle of consciousness, all that your eye or ear or touch has sensed, must go on toward the supreme, individually. I mean this literally. Every stone, the component parts of which are unseen by you, the plant that is bursting into bloom on

Joan's table, the little cat that used to curl about your neck as she lay on your shoulder, all travel toward the supreme degree as individuals.

"There have gone on toward supremacy individual consciousnesses that on the earth-plane were of a degree now passed away from earth forever. There were, for example, forms of prehistoric man, of which you know nothing save as science builds an imaginary body around the meager parts it excavates. The consciousness of those individuals has gone on; the consciousness of certain of those individuals has reached supremacy. Everything develops, until in supremacy each individual is the equal of every other. And when all of consciousness is supreme there will be but one degree."

"What about the supremacy of evil?" I asked.

"Supreme consciousness is the height of positiveness," replied Stephen. "There can be nothing negative in the supreme."

He continued:

"The fact of supreme consciousness, I think, is not beyond your conception. Truly, the world has had its vision of the supreme. The world has known the quality of him the ages have called the Christ. That quality was so near the height that, quantitatively fulfilled— and it was so fulfilled—it attained, at earth graduation, the height. But, though the fact of supremacy is within your conception, its attributes, as I have indicated, are what you on your earth-plane cannot imagine, any more, indeed, than I can.

"I have never been to what an Oriental, in his hypothetical way, might call the seventh heaven. From it I, like you, am many graduations removed. Therefore my information is limited to that which I have been told here by those nearer supremacy

227

than myself, and to those things I have learned out of the very nature of my qualitatively free existence. And such knowledge of supreme attributes as I have I cannot make clear to you; earth lacks terms for conveying my thoughts. Will you ask questions?" •

"You hold," I said, "that all is evolutional up to the supreme, yet you say the supreme itself is not reborn. How do you explain the contradiction between the becoming of things less than supreme and the fixed state of supremacy itself?"

"The supreme is the ultimate," Stephen answered. Silence a moment—then he added, "There is one with me here who says that the supreme may evolute within itself."

"Stephen," I asked, "is the nature of the supreme logical or ethical?"

"Logical," he replied, "and, I think you will agree with me, ethical as well, as it is the supreme of all that you know."

"The supreme," I asked, "is subjective only? It possesses no world corresponding to what we term the objective?"

"Why do you say that?" Stephen said. "What you call the objective world is made up of consciousnesses other than yourself and the attributes of those others. The supreme, I have told you, is pluralistic, and it is possessed of attributes."

With such questions I but delayed the bigger query that was in my mind, though, for that matter, Stephen already had answered that query time and time again.

I said at last, "The supreme of consciousness exists now—"

"Like the core of an apple," Stephen interjected.

"And," I went on, "millions of years ago there was no life as earth now knows it. Hence there was a time when the supreme did not exist. Yet we have long believed that there existed, even before the dawn of life, a God, a being of omnipotence, perfection, changelessness, and that by Him life was made. Shall we dismiss that always existing God of always existing supremacy?"

And Stephen answered, "We must."

"Anyway," I ventured, "science already has shaken that conception of deity from its pedestal."

"Surely," said Stephen. "Yet science now must learn that, though understanding of material law has routed the dogmas of religion, spirituality remains unannihilated. Science must learn not simply to destroy, but also to construct. It must replace the God it destroys with a better. For God is. Men find God in their hearts; He is not to be denied.

"Consciousness is its own creator, its own savior. But, if you will, translate the supreme degree of consciousness as God. And if you are shocked by the thought that supremacy was not always existent, except as a potentiality, consider that consciousness, being the all, is time itself."

I asked for more detail concerning time and a word relative to space.

"Time and space," said Stephen, "are attributes of consciousness. Consciousness, being a pluralistic oneness in process of evolution, is, as your every-day experience tells you, necessarily a thing of relationships. Those relationships that are evolutional you know temporally. Those that result from the pluralistic character of the whole you know spatially. As attributes of consciousness time and space are real, as reason or will or form is real. But time and space do not mean to you what they mean to an insect. Nor do they mean to supreme consciousness what they mean to you. There you have parallelism. Supreme consciousness;—"

Stephen hesitated, then spoke this solitary word, "Inadequate."

"Discouraged, Stephen?" I asked.

"No," he answered. "There can be no discouragement. But the want of words to make clear to you the vision of the supreme that I have gained here is, to say the least, impressive. The supreme of consciousness is made up of individual supreme consciousnesses. As a loaf of bread can be separated into crumbs, each crumb being in quality the equal of every other crumb, so is supremacy a whole of parts. Yet it is a whole, just as the loaf of bread is a whole. Consciousness supreme is oneness supreme."

XXIX

WILL

THE free will of man, my dear sir, is the one attribute that is wholly and distinctly his own. Degrees of consciousness nearing man have something that approaches reason, something even closer to memory, and are possessed of attributes comparable to the five senses. But animal life does not have free will. This is man's peculiar possession. Because of free will man is man."

It was not Stephen who spoke. It was the professor. Heretofore the professor's messages had been brief, consisting of occasional comment on this or that statement of Stephen's or on some remark made by Joan or myself. But now, with that ancient obstacle, free will, up for formal consideration, the professor led the discourse.

"The will of man," he went on, "is hampered not even by his quality, be it low. It is as free for all men as for one. But for an individual to live up to his quality he must use his will in the gathering of quantity. Not to use the freedom of one's will is to deny one's self of self. Free will constitutes every man's opportunity, permitting him to control the degree of consciousness he attains on graduation.

"Take a negro servant of—may I still call it our own South? — uneducated, uncultured, unrefined in his tastes, happy with little, undistressed by the lack of creature comforts, unappreciative even of the fact that he is undistressed. Personally I have known such a one, through the use of his free will, to develop quantity most disproportionate to his quality. I have known men of high quality endowment, with talent, with the world's wealth and the attainments that such wealth could command; and I have known these men to go through the entire span of their earth existence and by the use of their own free will develop not one-tenth of the actual quantity that some old Southern uncle had gathered unto himself.

"Do not make any mistake about the freedom of man's will. It is his to use, and use develops it, just as exercise develops the muscles of one's body. Disuse deadens it. And as to the purpose of free will make no mistake. For it is only as the free will carries out the behests of that still, small voice, man's quality of consciousness, that the lessons of earth are finished, the book closed, and a wider worlds a greater freedom and more perfect understanding attained upon graduation."

After a moment of silence the professor asked if I had ever studied James's psychology. And when I answered that I had skimmed through it in school he asked, "Where is the book?"

"My copy disappeared long ago," I answered. "Joan has a copy, but—"

"Look behind Moliere," said the professor. "I want you to read me James's definition of will. We shall see if one who is a dead man can improve on it."

I found the book—as the professor had suggested—hidden behind the Moliere volumes. I was surprised. Some months before, in order to make shelf-room, I had packed the few college texts Joan and I had kept, in a box for storage. I was sure I had put the James text in that box.

I signaled Joan for interruption of the communication.

"Where is your copy of James's psychology?" I asked, keeping the book from her view.

"I am sure I don't know," Joan answered.

"Is it in the box I packed for storage?"

"Probably," she said, "though I don't know just what books you put into that box."

"Do you remember putting the psychology behind Moliere?"

"No," replied Joan. "But why do you think I did?"

When I related what had happened Joan said she might have placed the James book behind the others. She could not remember having done so, yet she was unable to say positively that she had not.

The incident of the professor's apparent knowledge of the whereabouts of Joan's copy of James's psychology furnishes an excellent illustration of the possibility, if not the definite actuality, of subconscious memory assuming the guise of spiritistic communication. I should quote here, however, a remark once made by Stephen. He said: "During mental communication I have access to Joan's subconscious knowledge. You might vaguely mention to me a fact with which I was unfamiliar; if Joan knew of the details of that fact she could inform me of them."

When communication was resumed the professor repeated his request that I read him James's definition of will. I read the following:

"Desire, wish, will, are states of mind everybody knows, and which no definition can make plainer. We desire to feel, to have, to do, all sorts of things which at the moment are not felt, had, or done. If with the desire there goes a sense that attainment is not possible, we simply wish; but if we believe that the end is in our power, we will that the desired feeling, having, or doing shall be real; and real it presently becomes, either immediately upon the willing or after certain preliminaries have been fulfilled."

"Well," said the professor, "I think that is a pretty comprehensive assertion, even according to my wider knowledge. I would add that the will of man is the highest servant of both his mind and soul. Superior to reason, it is the active manifestation of the voice of his quality. Metaphysically, it is the visible, outward sign of his innermost invisible thought; ethically, it results in what is known as morality; practically, it is the achievement of high quantity."

"But," I said, "our choice frequently seems determined for us. It appears that we do many things not out of the freedom of our will, but as effect of causes over which we have no control."

"Do you remember," the professor replied, "how in seeking to understand the pluralistic nature of the oneness of consciousness you found solution of your difficulties in the thought that experience is broader than reason? Experience likewise testifies to the freedom of man's will. Every man feels that his will is free. Face him with alternatives and bid him choose. He will admit that his choice is influenced by factors external to himself, and by his past and his hopes for the future. Yet he feels always that actual decision rests simply with himself."

"But," I said, "if free will is a fact, certainly reason can be made to see it as such."

"Evolution," the professor answered, "when considered in the light of Stephen's law of parallels, makes free will clear even to reason. Take chemical affinity. The action of one chemical on another is absolutely determined, yet it is action. Now take an infinitely low form of life—the ameba. So closely is the ameba related to mere chemical reaction that its agency seems quite chemical. Yet science recognizes it as more than simply are action; it is life. Go up the scale of life now. More and more the living thing differentiates itself from chemical activity until at last instinct, a really understandable parallel to man's will, is reached. And then, especially in the domestic animals, we find instinct of a still higher order, yet it is not will; the stray dog pauses at a corner, then takes the route home, led by instinct arid a form of memory that amounts almost to reason. The dog wills not. At last man is reached.

"What is the difference between the instinct which leads the dog to act and the will that prompts the action of a man? Is it not apparent that the dog's urge is conditional, not so conditional as chemical reaction, yet responsive for the most part only to stimuli, while man's will, far from being prodded into activity, is spontaneous, possessed of an actual freedom.

"Freedom, in other words, is evolved by consciousness out of that which was less than freedom, and thereby consciousness becomes man. Deny the freedom of a man's will and immediately you have denied man's very being. Man, in truth, can be defined only in terms of free will. He is the free-will degree of consciousness.

"But not always does man's will choose wisely. The animal following its instinct seldom errs; a chemical reaction never errs. Not always does

235

man's reason guide his will correctly. It is not his will that fails of freedom, but his reason that fails of wisdom."

When the professor had finished Stephen came and said:

"It is because your wills are free that fortune-telling is futile. Except as I judge of your quality I do not know what you, in the freedom of your own will, will do to-morrow."

"But," I asked, "doesn't supremacy know all?"

"You can study the causes at work in a given situation," Stephen answered, "and with more or less accuracy predict the effect that will result from those causes. So do we here, though our more complete knowledge gives us greater accuracy of foresight. And as we approach supremacy, as the causes and their relations one with another become clearer, farther and farther we are able to foresee. It is not otherwise on earth; the quality that is high anticipates the happening that the quality that is low cannot see until it has actually developed. In supremacy the scroll is quite unrolled. Knowing all, supremacy can foresee all. But even supremacy's knowledge of the 'will-be' is founded on understanding of the 'was' and 'is.' The parallel between prevision on my plane and on yours holds even in the supreme degree.

"In any case, remember that the will, the act, is yours. What would it profit a man if, with his steps charted out for him one by one, he followed them blindly, granted supremacy itself has made the chart? The individual consciousness must vision its own future and itself win toward that future."

XXX

GOOD AND EVIL

STEPHEN," I asked, "what of good and evil?"

"Christ," answered Stephen, "said, 'Resist not evil.' Frankly, when I was on earth and used to go to Sunday-school, this saying of Christ's was a thing that puzzled me. For as a small boy there were so many things I was told I must not do that at least half of my time was taken in resisting the temptation of them. It may not be a psychological fact of much dignity, but certainly it is an every-day boy fact that the things a youngster is told he ought not to do immediately become the only anticipatory joys of existence. When I grew older and came to an understanding that gave me the power to differentiate between the so-called good and evil of the world, I confess that even then evil had a peculiar attraction. It was the unexplored country.

"I remember one day in freshman Bible class our instructor's taking up Christ's phrase. This instructor was a man of more than one glimpse. He not only perceived truths, but he joyously lived them. He was so busy doing the things that were positive—positive for the upbuilding of his own character, positive jn the way of example—that I don't believe he ever had time for a negative thought. I remember he told us that these old words, 'resist not evil,' meant simply that the devil still finds work for idle hands to do.

"Since I have come here I have grown to realize what the scientists of earth have known, in their hearts at least, for some time—namely, that there is no actual evil, just as there is no actual state of cold or actual state of darkness. Cold is merely the absence of heat; darkness the absence of light. Evil is the non-development of good."

Now it was the very day Stephen began his discussion of good and evil—or, as he says, the negative and the positive—that Joan had asked me to bring home to her a certain package; and I was well on my homeward way that evening when it occurred to me I had left Joan's package lying on my desk. A shower was coming up and I was umbrella-less.

Here, then, was a genuine evil, nothing of far-reaching concern, yet to me an all-round annoyance. What was the evil? Was it not, to use Stephen's word, simply a negative? I had forgotten something I should have remembered.

When memory of the package did come it was accompanied by two thoughts. The first of these was that it would be a task to walk back through the rain. The other was that Joan had planned on my bringing the package, and, unless she received it, her affairs for the next day would be put awry. A momentary debate went on within me. Then, in the exercise of my free will, I faced about, trudged off through the downpour, got the package, and so preserved Joan's morrow. And I had the pleasant realization of having overcome evil. But had I resisted evil? Certainly I had not. The incident, slight though it is, seems illustrative, from the viewpoint of Stephen's philosophy, of all those things that the world calls evil and of that saying of Christ's that enjoins non-resistance.

There are many persons, of course, who, misinterpreting the meaning of Christ's injunction, not only refuse to resist evil, but also to fight for the good. They miss the entire point; for, except as one does fight for the positive, he must inevitably fritter his energies away resisting the very negatives to which he fancies he is closing his eyes.

"Is this not so, Stephen?" I asked,

"But surely," answered Stephen. "It is the men who fight for the positive that count. They are the men who in business realize the hopelessness of fighting against inefficiency and the necessity of fighting for efficiency. They are the men who in medicine remove the cause of an epidemic. They are the soldiers who enthrone right, by force if need be.

"Truly there is little new in what I tell you of the negative character of evil. The scientist knows even more than is on the surface of the bald statement that what the world calls evil is only lack of development. He knows, for example, that as evolution progresses negatives disappear and positives rule; he knows that the goal is development so complete that there will be neither negative nor positive, but simply the height of development."

Well, it may be, as Stephen says, that his view of good and evil contains little that is new. Yet—for me, at least—he has made the world's sorrow easier of understanding; and, I think, he has pointed out a way to make it easier of alleviation.

Let me illustrate. Rather blindly men have been preaching for a space of years that the criminal should not be punished, but given instead an opportunity to assume a right relation with society.

Frequently the voice of the preacher has been drowned by those who, demanding an eye for an eye, would fight negatives with negatives. And the preacher himself has not always been coherent.

Stephen classifies human negatives in this fashion:

1. That lack of development which is qualitative; in other words, that fundamental lack which distinguishes a high degree of consciousness from a low degree.

2. That lack of development which is quantitative, the quality in the individual case being good, but put to limited use by the free will of its possessor.

Of the first of these Stephen said: "Men and women of low quality are prone to evil as the sparks fly upward. Yet compare them with persons of high degree and what do you find? No difference in kind. All are simply men and women. The one class has attained a higher degree of development—that is the only difference. Thousands of years ago the men and women of your present who appear most negative would have appeared most positive. And even to-day, if you were to set them down in a tribe of cannibals, they would by comparison shine as saints.

"What is society's duty to those whose quality in contrast to the mean of society's consciousness seems negative and evil? Surely that part of the whole of consciousness represented by men and women of high degree must aid parts of the whole lower than itself in finding opportunity to develop quantity. And this opportunity should be broader than any the low degree, unaided, could create for itself.

"Nonetheless you should remember that low degrees are low. Though society shall not wreak revenge upon the criminal of low quality, it must often assume full responsibility for him, to the extent, if necessary, of life control."

Of those negatives which result from failure on the part of an individual to develop quantity in accordance with his quality, Stephen said:

"The person of high quality whose quantity is negative may be the victim of economic conditions. Or he may be the victim of a will weak from disuse or misguided by false reasoning.

"That day should be hastened when economic conditions shall be positive. In the mean time the victim of economic negatives should, when his evil-doing overtakes him, be aided, not crushed. When faulty volition brings a person of good quality into collision with society the problem is individual in its solution; guidance is needed."

"Stephen," I said, "the other day two young fellows, convicted of murder, were executed. What of capital punishment?"

"I know of those boys," answered Stephen. "One was—he still lives—a primary grade of human consciousness. The other was and is of good quality, but undeveloped quantity. Both should have been given their opportunity on earth to develop that degree of quantity which would have fulfilled their quality. He who was of primary human consciousness would have found his best opportunity under constant restraint—life-imprisonment you call it—a harsh term, and often, as you practise it, a harsher thing. Had the other young fellow, he of good quality, been given opportunity and help, together with increasing freedom as he took advantage of that help, he might have been saved for the gathering unto himself of much quantity."

Is it clear? Do Stephen's words mean what I think they mean? The reformer in his fervor has been tempted to pamper the criminal. The conservative has shouted, "Vengeance is mine." Is it not merely a case of both being right and both being wrong? Is it not the glory of Stephen's message that the truth can be separated from the untruth?

"Stephen," I said, "there is no hell?"

"But there is," he answered. "The freewill degree of consciousness is its own judge. We make our own hell. Yet to the soul imprisoned in the torment of its own regrets, its own remorse, its own repentance, I say this: Regret is vain. The past is dead; it cannot leave a scar, big or little, on that quality of consciousness which has been vouchsafed an individual. 'Rust cannot empale the quality of gold.'

"But if you fail, it is the law of consciousness that in that failure you shall not find rest. You are on the road to supremacy; there is no turning back. You must reach supremacy, and by your own effort. True, there is a leavening whereby the victory of each part is the victory of the whole; yet the failure of each part is the failure of the whole. 'You are your brother's keeper' takes on a new meaning.

"And now to go back to the phrase that so puzzled me in my boyhood, 'Resist not evil.' There came one after the Master, a follower of His and a great philosopher, who summed up Christ's philosophy in four words. And these four words are the summing up of this particular portion of the old, yet new, statement of truth it has been given me to bring you, 'Overcome evil with good.'"

XXXI

SERVICE

"WHY is it, Joan," I asked my wife one evening, "that you no longer complain of the impracticalness of Stephen's theories?"

"They no longer strike me as impractical," she answered.

"But," I said, quoting words of her own, "if when we die we don't, the fact is just so."

"And that's true," she answered. "But in the mean time we must live here. From Stephen I have learned something about workaday living."

A night or two later Stephen reached the climax of what it has pleased him to call his revelation, and that climax did, indeed, concern the most practical of workaday matters —service.

"The one excuse for living," Stephen said, "is leavening through service. "I bring you this fact, that spiritual laws parallel material laws, both being degree expressions of the one reality. Take an engine, and note how the service of the given cog to its neighbor is really service to the entire machine. The cog is a good cog only as it serves the whole of which it is a part. In as far as it pursues ends unrelated to the purposes of the entire machine it is a bad cog. Now, if you will apply your knowledge of the cog— literally—to the spiritual adjustments in the midst of which you live, you will have learned the truth.

"The scheme of things is illustrated by man's organizations, which are but unconscious glimpses of the all-embracing oneness. Take an efficient business concern. The departments are intrusted to various heads. Under the supervision of these department heads further details are intrusted to individual employees. Each of these individual employees is absolutely responsible for his given work. If he fails, he lowers the worth and perfection of the business as a whole.

"Now suppose consciousness is the business; the degrees of consciousness, the heads of departments; the employee, the individual developer of quantity or quality, according to the plane. You can see that perfection of the whole can be obtained only through the individual,

"Christ preached this, 'Inasmuch as ye have done it unto the least of these my brethren, ye have done it unto me.'

"Man through the centuries has gloried in this saying of Christ. Yet the literal truth contained in the words has by most men been only glimpsed. There is but one reality. There is but one 'me,' of which 'the least of these' and the greatest are but parts. Do it to another and you have done it to the whole; serve the whole of which you are a part and you serve yourself."

Stephen paused, and asked me to touch Joan's wrist. "Read Joan what I have said," he requested, "and say to her for me that my theories have sought, not only to make the survival of personality after death a reasonable thing, but also to make reasonable, in the light of assured survival, the ethical ideals mere faith has recommended to men."

And when I did as Stephen asked Joan said: "1 have demanded something practical. I think, Darby, Stephen has given it to me. If we are all just partners in the common business of a one reality, itself imperfect, but developing toward perfection, then the only really practical thing in the world is service."

And so in the end the practical Joan was satisfied.

"Stephen," I said, when communication was resumed, "Napoleon certainly developed much quantity. His difficulty must have been low quality."

"And why do you say that?" asked Stephen. "Because," I answered, "he gave so little of service."

"His quality could not have been low," replied Stephen, "considering the very great quantity he developed. What do you know of the purpose he served? Much you can know if you will trace the results that sprang from causes he set in motion. Much, perhaps, you will never know; the skeins of human organization are many, and it is difficult to trace a single thread."

Puzzled, I mentioned a contemporary, a great developer of quantity, who has seemed to climb to success over the shoulders of those weaker than himself.

"The system that produces such men," answered Stephen, "is bad—just as the French Revolution of itself was bad, yet from that bad much good has sprung. Understand, I do not approve of the many negatives in the character of men like Napoleon and him you have just mentioned. Yet there is sure to be much of the positive in them; hence they serve, despite their selfishness. The man you mention, your fellow-countryman and mine, at least has created work for many hands."

"Then," said I, "it would seem that service need not be proclaimed. One may serve without dedicating himself, as they say, to his fellow-men? One may serve unconsciously?"

"But surely," answered Stephen. "Take the scientist, cold, recluse, indifferent apparently to the humanity about him, but who gives his life for the sake of proving a new theory to add to the store of earth's knowledge. He has given of himself to the oneness of the body of the people, to the common knowledge of the generations. He has developed quantity; he has rendered service.

"Take the maker of a saucepan. In as far as that man makes a serviceable saucepan— though consciously he labors but for hire—he, too, in his degree gives himself to the oneness of the people. He, too, has developed quantity; he, too, has served.

"Listen! It is not the kind of service that matters. It is the service itself.

"Nor must service be patently what the world calls utilitarian. The writer of the great poem has just as surely done the whole of consciousness a service as the founder of a hospital. The artist, the musician, the builder of an ocean liner, or the maker of a saucepan, each has served.

"Man, in his emotional hypotheses, has lost sight of the divers kinds of service that the world requires. Happily these divers kinds of service spring quite naturally from the divers degrees of men. For it has been given to every soul to have a conception, termed by the Psalmist the still, small voice" (Stephen is in error here; it was Elijah who heard the still, small voice, not David), "of his individual place in the scheme of things and his individual aptness for developing and gathering unto himself that quantity which his endowment of quality, itself the voice, dictates. And yet—to the narrow interpretation of service that has been fostered by dogmatic teaching add the rush of modern life, add the luxuries that have become necessities, the false standards set for all men, whether they be able to measure up to them or not, and do you wonder that more than one man has closed his eyes to that inner sight and his ears to the inner call?

"Service is the badge of quality quantitatively fulfilled."

"Shall Christ's parable of the talents be cited?" I asked.

"But surely," answered Stephen. "You will recall how to one man there had been given five talents, to another two, and to another one. The gift to each was according to his responsibility.

"And you will remember how that man to whom, because his quality was high, there had been given five talents, fulfilled his quality. When he returned to his master not five talents, but ten, the master said, 'Well done, thou good and faithful servant; thou hast been faithful over a few things, I will make thee ruler over many things.'

"And likewise did the man to whom had been intrusted two talents prove a good and faithful servant, returning to his lord not two talents, nor yet ten, as his fellow-servant had done, but four. And he, too, was promised rulership over many things.

"But the third man to whom, because his quality was not so high as the others', there was intrusted but one talent, hid that talent in the earth, totally failing in quantitative development.

Him the master called a wicked and slothful servant.

"Now is it not plain that the degrees of quality were represented in each of these three men, that from each was expected service according to his individual qualitative degree? From the first man much was expected; and, as he delivered the goods, so he was rewarded. And the second man also made delivery of the goods, still according to quality. Though he served not so greatly as the first man, he served with equal faithfulness. But the third man failed even in the little that was justly expected of him. His service was faithless.

"Now I told you a bit ago that modern life has falsely set one standard for all men, whether they are able to measure up to it or not. What I meant is apparent from the parable. It is as though the man of one-talent responsibility had been expected to return to his master ten talents. It is as though ten talents were the sum of service expected from all men, regardless of whether their quality be of five-talent, two-talent, or one-talent capability.

"And so the emphasis of my speech to you regarding service is laid, not on the big service that the few may do, but on the small service that the many may do."

I took advantage of a pause to ask, "And if the ability be given a man to serve consciously, to efface himself and give greatly, dedicating his heart and mind and hand to a service unbounded, what then?"

"This, then," answered Stephen, "if such a one fail, greater is his failure than that of the man who hid his solitary talent, for greater is his achievement if he succeed. It is given to a man to render such service only because his quality has been reborn from a degree of consciousness that through ages of struggle has lifted itself out of unconscious recognition of the oneness of things into understanding. And if this man, himself at the ladder's top, chooses to ignore his opportunity to make the ascent easier for those still on the bottom rungs, he brings to consciousness on graduation only that which was vouchsafed him at birth—his quality. True, his quality, even so, is unempaled; but true also it is that consciousness sits judge of self, and still must the degree be reborn, until quantitatively fulfilled. Individually that man has lost the opportunity earth existence offered.

"But listen! King or beggar, each is a cog in the great wheel. The exhorter on the street corner, the martyr at the stake, the dispenser of wide charity, each gives to the whole of consciousness a gift no better than he who every day performs the simple, lowly task, immediately important in his individual existence. A deed of heroism by a man whose soul is fired with understanding means no more as done by that man than a dirty tramp's sharing of the half of his last loaf with a pal. Nor do such men claim heroism for great deeds. Rather they say: 'It was nothing. I saw the thing had to be done—so I did it.' And this is the point, their quality is such that they recognized the need.

"Service, the badge of quality quantitatively fulfilled, is the simple process of living fully in one's appointed place"

CONCLUSION—THROUGH A GLASS DARKLY

IF Stephen is real, if he is what he purports to be, then the probability is that the things he has told Joan and me are, in the main, true.

"In the main," I say; because, however truthful the general outline of Stephen's philosophy, the chance of error in detail must not be overlooked. Coloring, to use Stephen's own term, must be reckoned with.

By coloring we have thus far meant the unconscious distortion of a message by the receiving station. Are there other circumstances that make for inaccuracy of communication? There are, just as surely as a communicated thought requires a material medium of transmission.

Convinced, in the days of the ouija-board, that neither Joan nor I guided the tripod, our hands seeming rather to follow it, I asked Stephen for an explanation. He said:

"I confess my inability to make clear to you how this ouija-board is operated. Here, as elsewhere, your limited understanding sets bounds to the knowledge I can bring you. There is involved in communication a psychology and physics new to you concerning which I can tell you little, because of lack of earth terms."

Yet repeatedly I raised the question. At the risk of being none too coherent, I submit the following, which summarizes various remarks Stephen has made relative to the material medium employed in transmission of a message:

There is a refined form of energy, called by Stephen magnetic consciousness, through the medium of which he is able to impress his thought on Joan's subconscious mind, in some such fashion as I am able to impress my thought on her conscious mind through the medium of atmospheric vibration. But this, we have seen, is not enough; communication results only on release of Stephen's message from Joan's subliminal. The force used in the case of the ouija-board to release the message from the subconscious is the same force originally used to convey the message, though a transformed variety. And the transformation, Stephen has led us to believe, is accomplished by Joan's own subconsciousness.

Manifestly such a statement means little until such time as the scientist's physical experimentation discovers and defines the energy Stephen merely predicates. The statement is made here only for the purpose of suggesting the delicate physical adjustments that go to make the mechanism of communication—a mechanism beside which the fine adjustments of a telephone or wireless appear but gross affairs.

The success of telephone communication depends on the perfection of the telephonic mechanism. If the connection is imperfect, the message is confused. And so it is, Stephen says, with communication between persons on his plane and persons here on earth; the connection, so to speak, may be good, bad, or indifferent.

Therefore, the version of Stephen's philosophy that I have been able to record may contain inaccuracies not only because of mental coloring attributable to the receiving station, but also because of physical defects in what might be called the line of magnetic consciousness, over which Stephen, handicapped by "trouble," could but do his best to make himself understood.

Indeed, all conversation I have held with Stephen concerning the manner of communication, or the form of psychic phenomena generally, has tended to impress upon me how ever-present is the possibility of error as the result both of coloring and of defects in the mechanism of transmission.

I once asked if the word "control," as used in mediumistic parlance, stood for any actual fact.

"In a way, yes," Stephen answered. "A receiving station can take the message of a degree the equal of itself and, with less understanding, that of a degree higher than itself. It sometimes happens that high degrees here, hoping to be understood the better by an earth station of low degree, will convey a message through some one here of a degree close to the station's. But such messages are often greatly colored, like a story too frequently repeated.

"Many stations speak of their 'controls' and think that only the 'control' can communicate with them directly. This is, of course, an emotional hypothesis. You can understand now how it came about."

"Is the idea of materialization also an emotional hypothesis?" I asked.

"Not necessarily," Stephen answered. "There are two types of materialization. What might be called true materialization means simply that the range of the earth degree's vision has momentarily broadened, usually, but not always, under the stress of emotion or nervous excitement. We here have nothing to do with that; we are simply seen by the earth degree. But as a rule the interpretation the earth degree puts on the thing it has seen is a colored one.

"The other type of materialization is rather difficult for me to explain. There are certain degrees of men who are able to project the true form of their consciousness, of which I have spoken to you, in such a way that it becomes partially dissociate from their bodies. It is then seen as a type of matter, apart from the body as you know it. This projection is entirely physical or natural. We here do not cause it. We might, however, take note of its occurrence; and, if the person happened to be a receiving station, we might by impressing our thoughts on his subconsciousness control the appearance or look of the projected form. Such an undertaking would be so involved that no satisfactory result could be definitely predicted."

"How could you control the appearance of the projected form?" I asked.

"By controlling the thought of the person from which the form had been projected," Stephen answered. "The projection tends to shape itself to the cast of the projector's thought.

"Joan has spoken of our 'making pictures.' By this is meant that by taking thought I can alter the appearance of my material form. If it were possible for you to see me at this moment, I would seem to be dressed in clothes just as you are. That is the 'picture' I would make for your understanding, and, incidentally, I suppose, give you a misconception."

"What about table-tippings and raps?" I asked.

"These, too, are physical phenomena," Stephen replied, "resulting from partial projection of the true materiality of men's consciousness. These we here can and do use for the purpose of communication, just as we use the ouija-board.

"In mental communication the receiving station must constantly differentiate between his own thoughts and those of the communicator; failure to so differentiate results in coloring. Coloring of this sort is less likely when we utilize such obviously physical phenomena as raps and table-tippings. The difficulty here is that the degree exhibiting the physical phenomena is generally of relatively low understanding."

Another source of error lies in what Stephen calls "cross-currents." Occasionally messages have come that were not only meaningless to Joan and me at the time, but remained so. This happened more frequently in the days of the ouija-board than after the mental method was developed. Yet only recently a personality appeared that insisted on talking about "digging in the woods," the name "Cora" being associated with the "digging" phrase. Such communicators speak a word or two, and as suddenly as they came are gone; they may later reappear, but as a rule do not. In commenting on this sort of thing, Stephen has said:

"A wireless station often picks up messages not intended for it. In the same way our messages are often picked up by earth degrees for whom they are not intended. It sometimes happens in such cases that the receiving station gets parts of one communication jumbled up with parts of another. These cross-currents are unavoidable, and the coloring they cause is quite as annoying to us as to you."

I have reproduced these conversations not with the thought that they offer satisfactory explanation of the various psychic phenomena discussed. My purpose has been to suggest the complex possibility of inaccurate communication. If Stephen is real, Joan and I recognize the chance that not all of his speech, as recorded in this book, is necessarily as he would have it.

If Stephen is not what he purports to be, if he is, for instance, the bizarre creation of subconscious mind, then the things he has said must be judged wholly on their own merits.

Whatever he is, Stephen has stated a new argument for survival after death, new, at least, to Joan and me. And this argument in no way depends on Stephen himself being a personality that demonstrably has survived death. Briefly, it is this:

Evolution represents both qualitative and quantitative development. Yet all change or transformation effected in this world of ours, all earthly development, is quantitative; here no qualitative development occurs. Therefore the actuality of evolution can be explained only on the hypothesis that a world of qualitative development does exist.

Let me state the matter concretely. Evolution indicates, beyond any doubt now generally entertained, that man developed out of life less than man. Man constitutes a quality differing from that of his origin. How was the development of that new quality possible in this world which obviously fosters quantitative development only? Is there any escape from the assumption that there exists a world, or mode of being, that admits of qualitative development?

Or put the matter this way: Life, the general whole of living things, stretches back continuously, the theory of evolution indicates, to a less-than-life origin. How did life, in quality differing so radically from its non-life origin, come into being? As the result merely of quantitative development? This is impossible. Life is the result of a development both quantitative and qualitative. Yet, Stephen says, earth permits quantitative development only. If so, the fact of biological evolution forces us to predicate a mode or plane of existence that admits of qualitative development.

And thus Stephen's qualitative and quantitative analysis of consciousness offers a state, a somewhere, for the continuation of life after what men have called death.

But it may be asked: Granted the necessity of the qualitative plane, does it follow that the individual man enters the qualitative mode of being as an individual? May not qualitative development be the activity of cosmic, rather than individual, consciousness, personality as such being lost at death in the great reservoir of the whole?

Stephen's answer to the latter question has been, No. He points out that cosmic consciousness, conceived as the destroyer of individuality, is a thought contrary to all of man's experience. "Yet," he has added, "there is an element of truth in the theory. It is a monistic glimpse, colored by emotional reasoning."

Joan and I take this position: If the existence of the qualitative plane should prove to be really indicated, as Stephen says it is, knowledge would have been advanced greatly —simply as the consequence of men reasoning from the basis of things as they are. The new knowledge would definitely indicate some sort of survival after death. In seeking to determine the nature of that survival men could scarcely reject the basis of reasoning that already had profited them so much—things as they are here and now. If quantitative development is effected through individuality, why imagine qualitative development is otherwise brought about?

I have stated now what seems to Joan and me the fundamental point of Stephen's philosophy. Is his argument for survival reasonable in the light of men's already acquired knowledge, even though he himself may be other than a living dead man?

And now is his philosophy reasonable as a whole?

To be truly reasonable a philosophic system must not only present consistently such data as it takes into consideration; it must also be able consistently to incorporate any fact new to it. In other words, the reasonable philosophy is not merely a system, but a method.

Joan and I have found Stephen's philosophy a method. We call it a method because it seems to act as a harmonist in every instance where thought has taken opposite paths, each path, according to the mind that travels it, seeming to be the true one.

If, for example, you who read are a mechanist, you believe that the universe is the result solely of mechanical forces, that by mechanical forces it is operated, that you yourself as a part of the universe are a mechanism, intricate, yet for all that just so much machinery. Modern science has leaned, with some show of right, to this viewpoint.

Mechanism requires no God. The universe is, the mechanist asserts; its laws are. Jab a man with a pin and he winces; destroy the equilibrium of a tower and it falls. To explain either the wincing flesh or the tottering tower, there is need of no God outside the machine. In all that vast automaton called the universe there is neither design nor aim.

Mechanism furnishes a sure basis for science. It asserts the inviolability of physical law. Under its rule Joshua may command, but the sun will not heed. Drought-stricken lands may cry out to the Most High for rain, but the skies do not hear. At a certain temperature the vapors of the atmosphere will condense; then and not until then will precipitation occur. To expect otherwise is like heating water to 212° Fahrenheit and then relying on prayer to prevent its boiling. Mechanism exalts law and banishes superstition.

On the other hand, if you are a teleologist, you believe that the universe is the result of an intelligent plan, that an intelligence guides its operation, that you, a part of the universe, are yourself an intelligence capable of conceiving a plan and purposefully executing it. Religion, with great show of right, asserts this viewpoint.

To teleology there is indicated a supreme intelligence whose aims the universe carries out. Surely man did not plan the universe. Indeed, who planned man? God, the supreme architect of all, teleology answers. With God, says the teleologist, all things are possible. Primitive teleology believes God can make the rain to fall when and where He will. Nor is the modern teleologist daunted by the formulas of meteorology. Long have we known, says he, that God moves in a mysterious way His wonders to perform. If, in granting a prayer for rain, He chooses first to drop the temperature of the atmosphere, then condense its vapors, wherein has He lessened the marvel of His omnipotence?

Teleology exalts faith in moral and spiritual values and in the ultimate good. Also it invites ignorance and trembling superstition.

Here, then, are contradictory thoughts, mechanism and teleology, both of which appear to be true, but neither of which wholly satisfies.

Is Stephen's philosophy mechanistic? Yes. Consciousness is. It is all there ever was or will be. A blade of grass, obeying innate impulse, seeks the light. Human consciousness, impelled by just itself, seeks supremacy. The universe created and creates itself. There is no deus ex machina, no extramundane God.

Is Stephen's philosophy teleological? Most assuredly. Consciousness, the all, is a whole of parts. Each part is in process of development, and the degrees of development severally attained by the parts are many. In one degree behold the blindly struggling blade of grass. And then behold man, the free-will degree, who, though he lives in a mechanistic body, has achieved for his self of self the liberty of choice.

Men, it is true, do not always choose to choose. We are carried upward toward supremacy not altogether by choice, but partly by an inherent must. Yet, to quote Stephen:

"What a blessed philosophy, how superior to your old religion of damnation! How much more encouraging is the knowledge that somehow, somewhere, over a long road or a short one, that ultimate and supreme mansion in the house of consciousness holds a room for every soul!"

Which, now, in the light of man's own knowledge, is the most reasonable—the mechanist, the teleologist, or Stephen?

While you are thinking it over let me quote again from Stephen:

"Some persons reading this revelation might feel that prayer, which has been of comfort to so many of the human race, is without worth. This is far from true. The voiced longing of a man's soul must of necessity have effect upon that whole of which he is a part.

"I have told you that God is Consciousness, the whole. I have also told you that you might, if you wished, translate God as the Supreme Degree of Consciousness, for the Supreme of Consciousness is, in fact, what your old categorical definition of God states—love, love all-wise, all-knowing, all-free. Now if the Supreme be love, can the turning of the individual soul toward it be useless? Prayer, the result of a definite desire on the part of the highest degree of consciousness known to earth, will beyond doubt influence a degree as high as itself. How much the more will it influence a higher degree, to whom increased understanding has brought increased sympathy and increased freedom, increased power.

"To whom shall you pray? Call him God, Buddha, Mohammed. Cry to the Virgin Mary or the saints. It is all one—Consciousness, the Reality.

"If you have a task to perform and it is more than you can alone accomplish, you turn to your neighbor. And you say to him, 'Come and help me with my harvest and I in turn shall give my aid to you.' You know the result; the task is accomplished.

"So in prayer the individual soul, or the national soul, turns to the great, neighboring hosts, calling upon those who have gone on to the higher life and more perfect understanding, and asks aid. And if that aid asked is positive, if it is not evil, but good, consciousness in and of itself is lifted up, and like a friendly neighbor answers the prayer.

"Take the present world conditions. Germany prays. France, England, Belgium—the knee of each is bended. The individual prayers of Germany, the crying out of a broken heart for ease, for comfort in suffering, are heard. Germany's national prayer, the negative prayer of tyranny and vengeance—surely you know enough of the philosophy of the universe to realize that such a prayer, in the evolutional order of things, must go unanswered. But the prayer that asks for progress, for mercy, for development, for freedom, must have the same influence on the ultimate outcome as that exerted by the peculiar force you know as enthusiasm, which makes it possible for a handful of men to become victors over vast armies."

"Stephen, Stephen," I interrupted, "you are drifting into the contention that faith can remove mountains."

"Not drifting," Stephen answered, "but steering a course. I would have you understand that faith, the vision of things to be, does remove mountains—daily."

"Perhaps so," I argued. "But isn't it true, under the terms of your philosophy, that all positive things must come to pass, though man utter never a prayer?"

"It is a psychological fact," Stephen replied, "and because it is a psychological fact it is also a natural law, that just as surely as man can aid in the consummation of material forces, so, too, can he aid in the consummation of spiritual victories.

"There was with earth-consciousness once a great American who is reported to have said, in more wisdom than he knew, 'God helps those who help themselves.' Yet prayer, the outlet of the human heart, the individual cry for aid, is the recognition of the oneness of all things; and the

261

One answers. Moreover, formulation in words of a desire is of itself a definite aid in the attainment of the thing wished for. For a clear thought is a thing, a mighty thing, while a subconscious longing is only an emotion."

And now let us approach the contradictions of teleology and mechanism from a new angle. Are you a Stoic or an Epicurean?

If you regard this life as a vale of tears, an evil thing to be borne with bravely but in the bearing despised, you are a Stoic. Mortify the flesh, for it is vanity; be indifferent alike to pleasure and pain; and great will be your reward in the final summing up of things.

Contrariwise, if you believe that, because there is no final summing up of things, the satisfaction immediately at hand, however fleeting, should be seized, you are an Epicurean. Your shibboleth is, "Eat, drink, and be merry, for to-morrow we die." Pain the world holds, to be sure; well, then, avoid it. Pleasure, the advantage even of the moment, is the end and aim of life. Carpe diem. We'll be a long time dead.

Doubtless as your mood varies you are one day a Stoic and the next an Epicurean. For it is the very oddity of such irreconcilables as free will and determinism, teleology and mechanism, Stoicism and Epicureanism, that in both man recognizes truth. And it is the happiness and reasonableness of Stephen's philosophy that it fits into the truth of each.

With the Stoic Stephen asserts that the life earth knows is, as compared with the life beyond, dark and narrow. But with the Epicurean he asserts that it is a thing above price. For by reason of the opportunity earth life offers for quantitative development, we take to the future life the requisite of qualitative development.

But you say such an assertion is not new, except, perhaps, in the novelty of its form; for centuries Christianity has been preaching a like sermon. In reply to a similar statement by me, Stephen said:

"I only repeat the essentials of Christianity and make them understandable, so that men, having learned to ignore its dogmas, may exalt its truth. I seek only to make the creed of service, freedom, and immortality reasonable in the light of the knowledge men have acquired since Christ passed from their sight.

"Reread Christ's words. A little you will reject. Much you will accept—all in fact that is essential; and you will know the why and wherefore of your acceptance.

"Remember this: Christ is. He is in the world of men to-day just as truly, just as personally, as when He lived with men. He is more truly in your world to-day than then; for now He is supreme."

If Stephen is not Stephen, what of the Stephen method? Is it reasonable?

This Stephen of ours comes and says, "I wish you would take down this letter."

And here is the letter in part, intimately personal matter being withheld:

Dear Mother,—This story that I have told Darby and Joan, as they choose to call themselves, will, of course, come into your hands. . . . There are several things I want to say to you.

263

The first is I am. I am just as the book says I
am, free to work, free to succeed, free to love you
as I always did. Man's consciousness, which is the
creative genius of earth, is more potential than his
creations. The bridges we build and the books we
write live after us, so you say. That is true, but
what is truer is that we who created them live after
they have crumbled to dust.

Just this, dear mother: I live.

And the next thing I want to say to you is that I
know you wonder why it was not to you I came
instead of to Darby and Joan. This was because
you are not what we call a station. Just as all
people cannot be musicians and painters, so all
people do not have the peculiar quality that makes
it possible for us here to use them as
communicating stations. You have read the book.
You will know what I mean by this.

Earth still has much to learn of life; her eyes
are sealed to sights, her ears to sounds. But many
there are who have had great glimpses of the truth
that there is no real death, that death changes only
the form-attribute of consciousness, and that
consciousness itself, the you of you and the me of
me, goes on into a more wonderful development,
where all the dreams we have dreamed and all our
heart's desires and longings are fulfilled. ... .

I am with you, following you from room to room
as I used to do, longing for your smile. You must
smile again. . . I am only here, just gone into a
new life, a freer country, the same place that you
are coming to.

With all my love, "stephen."

And here is another letter lately dictated by
Stephen:

Dear Darby And Joan,—I want to thank you for your patient work with me all these long months. I want to thank you for your tolerance of mind, and even your natural curiosity, that allowed you to overcome your skepticism as to that in which you did not believe and which you did not understand.

The work has been trying and long. But I am sure you will feel repaid in the quietude it may bring to even a few.

You have told me that my philosophy has taken from you all fear; that alone is worth while. Fear is the greatest enemy of the human mind. It causes more suffering than any other one thing. This, the banishing of fear, is what I want to do for others besides yourselves; this is why, in the hour of earth's hideousness, I was allowed to tell you these truths.

I am not good at putting things. So in closing I shall just say—that I am your friend, that I shall always be with you, and that you will be with me.

Faithfully yours, "stephen."

And now it is scarcely to be supposed that Joan and I have passed through the experience this book relates without having formed a definite opinion as to whether Stephen is or is not Stephen. It is one thing to say that during the experience our opinion shifted, now denying Stephen's reality, now affirming it. It would be quite another thing for us to assert that this shifting opinion failed in the end to stabilize itself. To withhold that final belief from you, the reader, would be unfair. So here it is.

Joan and I have formed a definite belief in Stephen's reality.

We believe Stephen is real, not because of the tests, convincing as they have been; for these, it is conceivable, might be explained away. That the terms of his philosophy should have come to us as though out of the air, with us ignorant of their meaning until Stephen elaborated them into a connected and dignified metaphysical system, seems a test unlikely, so far as we are concerned, to be explained away. Yet granted it were—still would Joan and I be compelled to accept the reasonableness of Stephen's message. And that the philosophy should be reasonable and the phenomenon a deception is a contradiction which, to use Stephen's words, Joan's mind and mine are not "nimble enough" to entertain.

THE END

About Linda Pendleton

Linda Pendleton has written in a variety of genres: nonfiction, mystery novels, comic book scripting, and screenplays. She coauthored nonfiction and fiction with her late husband, renowned author, Don Pendleton, (known as "the father of the Action/Adventure genre") including the popular nonfiction books, *To Dance With Angels,* and *Whispers From the Soul.* Her other nonfiction books include *A Walk Through Grief: Crossing the Bridge Between Worlds; Three Principles of Angelic Wisdom; A Small Drop of Ink; As Light as A Feather; Angelic Whispers of Love; Metaphysics of the Novel* with Don Pendleton; *The Cosmic Breath* with Don Pendleton; *Soul Expressions, Poetry Collection Linda Pendleton and Don Pendleton.*

Linda's fiction works include *The Unknown, A Novel;* the *Catherine Winter Private Investigator* Series: *Shattered Lens* and *Fractured Image; Corn Silk Days, Iowa, 1862; Sound of Silence; Roulette, The Search for the Sunrise Killer* by Don and Linda Pendleton; and a novelette, *The Masquerading Cowboy.*

Don and Linda Pendleton adapted and scripted Don Pendleton's first book in *The Executioner* Series, *War Against the Mafia* to Comics and following her husband's death, Linda adapted and scripted the second *Executioner, Death Squad* to Comic Graphic novel.

She has authored two online nonfiction E-Courses, *Journey to the Heart,* and *Healing Whispers.* Recently published E-books: *A Loving Presence; The UFO Phenomena: The Cosmic SOS;* and *How Thin the Veil!: 150 Years of Spiritualism.*

A native Californian, Linda is a member of The Authors Guild, and The Authors League. She has won several awards for her books. Although most of her time is devoted to her love of writing, she also enjoys the exploration of her family's genealogical roots.

Linda's Websites:
www.lindapendleton.com
www.todancewithangels.com
www.bunchofebooks.com

CPSIA information can be obtained
at www.ICGtesting.com
Printed in the USA
LVHW110547141120
671648LV00002BA/191